# A Workbook in Phonology

# THE INTERNATIONAL PHONETIC ALPHABET

## (revised to 1993, corrected 1996)

### Consonants (Pulmonic)

|  | Bilabial | Labiodental | Dental | Alveolar | Postalveolar | Retroflex | Palatal | Velar | Uvular | Pharyngeal | Glottal |
|---|---|---|---|---|---|---|---|---|---|---|---|
| Plosive | p b |  |  | t d |  | ʈ ɖ | c ɟ | k ɡ | q ɢ |  | ʔ |
| Nasal | m | ɱ |  | n |  | ɳ | ɲ | ŋ | N |  |  |
| Trill | ʙ |  |  | r |  |  |  |  | R |  |  |
| Tap or flap |  |  |  | ɾ |  | ɽ |  |  |  |  |  |
| Fricative | ɸ β | f v | θ ð | s z | ʃ ʒ | ʂ ʐ | ç ʝ | x ɣ | χ ʁ | ħ ʕ | h ɦ |
| Lateral fricative |  |  |  | ɬ ɮ |  |  |  |  |  |  |  |
| Approximant |  | ʋ |  | ɹ |  | ɻ | j | ɰ |  |  |  |
| Lateral approximant |  |  |  | l |  | ɭ | ʎ | L |  |  |  |

Where symbols appear in pairs, the one to the right represents a voiced consonant. Shaded areas denote articulations judged impossible.

### Consonants (Non-Pulmonic)

| Clicks | Voiced implosives | Ejectives |
|---|---|---|
| ⊙ Bilabial | ɓ Bilabial | ' Examples: |
| ǀ Dental | ɗ Dental/alveolar | pʼ Bilabial |
| ǃ (Post)alveolar | ʄ Palatal | tʼ Dental/alveolar |
| ǂ Palatoalveolar | ɠ Velar | kʼ Velar |
| ǁ Alveolar lateral | ʛ Uvular | sʼ Alveolar fricative |

### Other Symbols

ʍ Voiceless labial-velar fricative

w Voiced labial-velar approximant

ɥ Voiced labial-palatal approximant

ʜ Voiceless epiglottal fricative

ʢ Voiced epiglottal fricative

ʡ Epiglottal plosive

ɕ ʑ Alveolo-palatal fricatives

ɺ Alveolar lateral flap

ɧ Simultaneous ʃ and X

Affricates and double articulations can be represented by two symbols joined by a tie bar if necessary.

k͡p t͡s

### Vowels

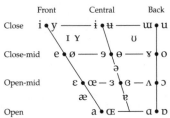

Where symbols appear in pairs, the one to the right represents a rounded vowel.

### Diacritics

Diacritics may be placed above a symbol with a descender, e.g. ŋ̊

| ̥ Voiceless | n̥ d̥ | ̤ Breathy voiced | b̤ a̤ | ̪ Dental | t̪ d̪ |
|---|---|---|---|---|---|
| ̬ Voiced | s̬ t̬ | ̰ Creaky voiced | b̰ a̰ | ̺ Apical | t̺ d̺ |
| ʰ Aspirated | tʰ dʰ | ̼ Linguolabial | t̼ d̼ | ̻ Laminal | t̻ d̻ |
| ̹ More rounded | ɔ̹ | ʷ Labialized | tʷ dʷ | ̃ Nasalized | ẽ |
| ̜ Less rounded | ɔ̜ | ʲ Palatalized | tʲ dʲ | ⁿ Nasal release | dⁿ |
| ̟ Advanced | u̟ | ˠ Velarized | tˠ dˠ | ˡ Lateral release | dˡ |
| ̠ Retracted | e̠ | ˤ Pharyngealized | tˤ dˤ | ̚ No audible release | d̚ |
| ̈ Centralized | ë | ̴ Velarized or pharyngealized | ɫ |  |  |
| ̽ Mid-centralized | ě | ̝ Raised | e̝ | (ɹ̝ = voiced alveolar fricative) |  |
| ̩ Syllabic | n̩ | ̞ Lowered | e̞ | (β̞ = voiced bilabial approximant) |  |
| ̯ Non-syllabic | e̯ | ̘ Advanced tongue root | e̘ |  |  |
| ˞ Rhoticity | ɚ a˞ | ̙ Retracted tongue root | e̙ |  |  |

### Suprasegmentals

ˈ Primary stress

ˌ Secondary stress

ˌfoʊnəˈtɪʃən

ː Long eː

ˑ Half-long eˑ

˘ Extra-short ĕ

| Minor (foot) group

‖ Major (intonation) group

. Syllable break ɹi.ækt

‿ Linking (absence of a break)

### Tones and Word Accents

| Level |  | Contour |  |
|---|---|---|---|
| e̋ or ˥ | Extra high | ě or ˩˥ | Rising |
| é or ˦ | High | ê ˥˩ | Falling |
| ē ˧ | Mid | e᷄ ˦˥ | High rising |
| è ˨ | Low | e᷆ ˩˨ | Low rising |
| ȅ ˩ | Extra low | e᷈ | Rising-falling |
| ↓ Downstep | | ↗ Global rise | |
| ↑ Upstep | | ↘ Global fall | |

# A Workbook in
# PHONOLOGY

Iggy Roca
and
Wyn Johnson
*University of Essex*

BLACKWELL
*Publishers*

First published 1999

Reprinted 2000

Blackwell Publishers Ltd
108 Cowley Road
Oxford OX4 1JF
UK

Blackwell Publishers Inc.
350 Main Street
Malden, Massachusetts 02148
USA

*British Library Cataloguing in Publication Data*

A CIP catalogue record for this book is available from the British Library.

*Library of Congress Cataloging-in-Publication Data*

Roca, Iggy.
A workbook in phonology / Iggy Roca and Wyn Johnson.
p.    cm.
Includes bibliographical references and index.
ISBN 0–631–21394–5
1. Grammar, Comparative and general—Phonology Problems, exercises, etc. I. Johnson, Wyn. II. Title.
P117.R63   1999
414—dc21                                         99–12252
                                                      CIP

Typeset in 10 on 12 pt Sabon
By Graphicraft Limited, Hong Kong
Printed and bound in Great Britain by MPG Books Ltd, Bodmin, Cornwall

This book is printed on acid-free paper

To all our students, past, present and future

# Contents

# Preface

*A Workbook in Phonology* has been written as an accompanying volume to the coursebook *A Course in Phonology*, in order to provide readers with further exercise material. Because of that, references are made to chapters and sections of *A Course in Phonology*, occasionally throughout the text and systematically in the Exercise Cross-Reference Table. Despite this, this workbook is a self-contained work, and may be used in conjunction with other teaching books or by itself.

The 104 exercises contained in this book are organized in blocks corresponding to the sections of chapter 20 of *A Course in Phonology*. As much as possible, the exercises are arranged in order of difficulty within each block. The first section contains exercises in phonetics and, in particular, transcription exercises, aimed at giving a good grounding in the IPA alphabet. The second section covers the first four phonology chapters of *A Course in Phonology*, and provides practice in the manipulation of phonological data. Subsequent sections, again corresponding to the sections of chapter 20 of *A Course in Phonology*, offer practice in syllables, stress, tone, the phonology/morphology interface, phonological domains, features and underspecification, and derivational theory. The final section of the book contains exercises in Optimality Theory. This section is longer, because of the growing importance and impact of Optimality Theory.

Many of the exercises are based on analyses in the literature, and we provide a key to the sources in the Exercise Cross-reference Table. Where no source is given, the data originate in the authors. It is worth bearing in mind that many of the analyses on which our sources are based are now old, and often out of date: readers should therefore be wary of going to the original source before attempting the exercise. In other cases, the source merely provides the data, with no analysis or discussion which would be of any use for the completion of the exercise.

It is well known that much of the literature exhibits a notorious lack of consistency regarding transcription, and it is not always immediately obvious exactly what some phonetic symbols mean in the practice of some writers. From time to time, we have felt confident enough to replace some of these idiosyncratic symbols with IPA symbols. When this is not so, we have had no choice but to retain the transcription of the source, although we have endeavoured to ensure that any confusion about the exact nature of the sound intended does not affect the exercise itself.

We have a firm belief that students will gain a greater insight into the concepts they are acquiring if they are able to put their fledgling knowledge into practice on real data. We also believe that problem-solving of this kind can be an illuminating and enjoyable experience, and we hope you will enjoy solving our puzzles as much as we have enjoyed compiling them. While you should find most of the exercises, if not all, easily manageable, given a reasonable amount of attention and thought, we will be pleased to answer queries from instructors at wyn@essex.ac.uk or iggy@essex.ac.uk

# I

# Phonetics

A reasonable grounding in articulatory phonetics is a prerequisite for the study of phonology, for the obvious reason that phonetics provides the substance that phonology organizes. Language sounds are basically divided into vowels and consonants, the latter in turn subdivided into obstruents and sonorants. The criterion for this division, and for its subdivisions, is that different types of sound hinder the exit of air to different degrees. Consonants are mutually kept apart by their place of articulation, their manner of articulation, the involvement or not of voice, and the involvement or not of nasality. In addition there are lateral and rhotic consonants. Vowels by definition do not obstruct the airflow in any way, but modulate it through the interaction of the tongue with the roof of the mouth, or palate. Voice is caused by the vibration of the vocal folds in the larynx, and nasality by the lowering of the velum. The ideal eight (or sixteen) basic vowels are known as the "cardinal vowels". The vowels of some languages approximate to the cardinal vowels more than the vowels of other languages. For better or worse, the vowels of English are not very "cardinal". Moreover, there is considerable variation in vowel realization throughout the English-speaking world. In order to study language sound we need to represent it in some durable medium. Spelling is often erratic, and language sounds are therefore conventionally encoded in phonetic symbols, of which the alphabet of the International Phonetic Association constitutes the standard and most widespread set.

# Articulation and Phonetic Symbols

a. Write down the IPA symbol which represents the following descriptions:

A voiced alveolar affricate
A voiceless palatal stop
A voiced glottal fricative
A voiced pharyngeal fricative
A voiceless uvular fricative
A voiceless dental fricative
A voiceless uvular stop
A voiced uvular fricative

b. Write down the description of the sound represented by the following IPA symbols:

[ɸ]  [ʃ]  [ẓ]  [ɟ]  [ʒ]  [b]  [ɢ]  [ɣ]

# Ghoti Words

In chapter 1 of *A Course in Phonology* we quote the remark by George Bernard Shaw (made in his spelling reformer capacity) that the word *fish* might equally be spelled as *ghoti* (i.e. *gh* as in *laugh*, *o* as in *women* and *ti* as in *nation*). By this token, the words listed below might each have been spelled in a number of different ways (in some cases, a large number of ways). First transcribe the words into IPA and then see how many possible spellings each could have, according to the apparent idiosyncracies of the English spelling system.

| | | | | | |
|---|---|---|---|---|---|
| sheaf | qualm | note | sign | jape | choose |
| fusion | daughter | chief | keep | mighty | chest |

## EXERCISE Incomplete Diagrams
## 1:3

The following illustrations are incomplete. Fill in the gaps in order to illustrate the sounds represented by the IPA symbols beneath each of them.

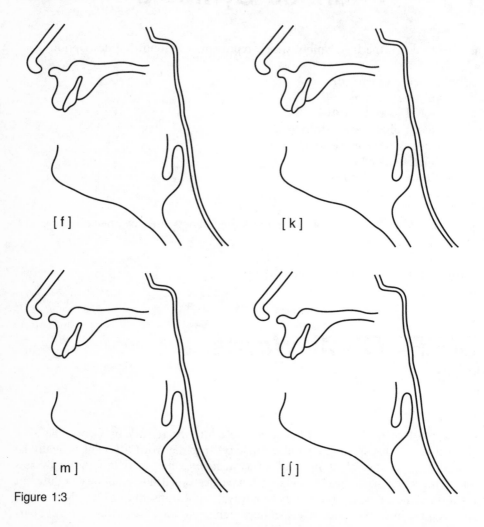

[ f ]          [ k ]

[ m ]          [ ʃ ]

Figure 1:3

# EXERCISE 1:4    Place and Manner of Articulation

Identify the place and manner of articulation of the sounds illustrated in the diagrams below, and provide phonetic symbols for the sounds. (NB: no voicing is indicated in the diagrams, so two symbols will need to be provided for each diagram.)

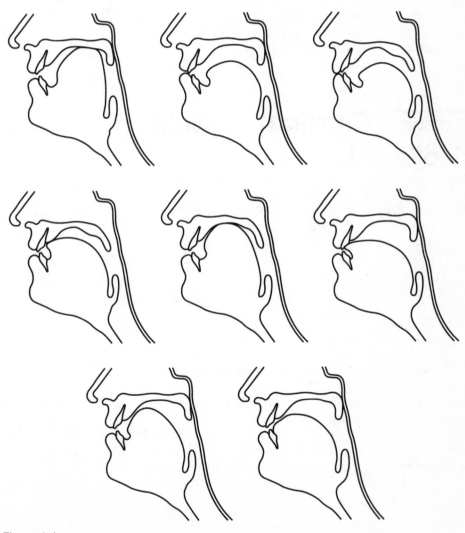

Figure 1:4

## EXERCISE 1:5   Glottal Stops and Flaps

Read the list of words below and say which of the orthographic *ts* can be pronounced as [ʔ] (a glottal stop) or [ɾ] (an alveolar flap), either in your accent or in an accent you are familiar with (their distribution will obviously differ according to accent). Try to elucidate the relative positions in the word of those *ts* which may be pronounced as [ʔ], [ɾ] or [t].

| Scotland | button | table | tatter | mistake |
|----------|--------|-------|--------|---------|
| market | cater | curtail | attract | tent |
| content | winter | static | attic | atlas |

## EXERCISE 1:6   Cardinal Vowels

(i)   Give descriptions of the eight primary and eight secondary cardinal vowels in terms of the following criteria:

Frontness
Backness
Highness
Lowness
Midness
Roundness

(ii)   Do these criteria distinguish all the vowels?

(iii)   Say what the difference is between the members of each of the following pairs relative to the criteria in (i):

a ~ e    o ~ ɔ    y ~ u    y ~ œ    y ~ i    i ~ ɛ    ɑ ~ u    ɑ ~ ɯ    ʌ ~ ɔ    ɒ ~ ɑ
ɤ ~ u    ɔ ~ ɛ    e ~ ɤ    i ~ ɑ    e ~ o    o ~ ʌ    a ~ ɑ    ø ~ e    ø ~ o    o ~ œ

# EXERCISE 1:7   English Vowels

We present four trapezoids, like those used to display vowels in chapters 5 and 7 of *A Course in Phonology*. Your task is to plot onto these figures the set of primary cardinal vowels in (a), the set of secondary cardinal vowels in (b), and those vowels emboldened in the words listed below in (c) and (d).

a.          b.

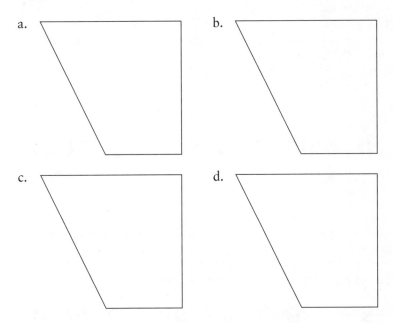

c.          d.

c.   bed   look   read   bad   soon   big   calm   call   gone   bun

d.   sigh   how   boy   day   dough

# EXERCISE
# 1:8
# Vowels

Provide IPA symbols and descriptions for the vowels highlighted in the following words in your own accent (e.g. [i] high front unrounded vowel):

| | | | | |
|---|---|---|---|---|
| rub | cook | Friday | cold | father |
| water | lake | tall | white | wide |
| loud | Jane | past | deep | bit |
| bet | bat | coat | late | choose |
| caught | cot | one | hour | bird |
| walk | dew | shore | sure | poor |

# EXERCISE
# 1:9
# RP Phonetic Transcription

Transcribe the following passage into normal English orthography (the symbol ' indicates the beginning of a stressed syllable):

ʃi 'left ə 'mɒnjumənt tu hə 'neɪm ɪn sɪnsɪ'næti ɜʊ'haɪɜʊ ən eks'tɹævəgnt 'bɪldɪŋ 'nɜʊn tə ðə 'ɹezɪdnts əv ðə 'sɪti əz 'tɪɒləps 'fɒli ən'tɪl ðeɪ 'faɪnli dɪ'mɒlɪʃt ɪt ɪn 'eɪtɪn'naɪntɪ'eɪt 'fɪfti jɪəz 'leɪtə. ði 'aʊtɹeɪdʒ ʃi pɹə'vɜʊkt ɪn 'evɹi 'steɪt əv ə'meɹɪkə 'baɪ ðə 'bʊk ʃi 'ɹɜʊt ə'baʊt ə'meɹɪkə 'aftə hə ɹɪ'tɜn tu 'ɪŋglnd 'meɪd hə 'dʒest əz wel 'nɜʊn. fə 'sevɹəl 'dekeɪdz 'pɪpl 'bɒt ðə 'bʊk ɪn 'ɔdə tu en'dʒɔɪ ðə 'fjuɹi ɪt en'dʒendəd ɪn ðəm. wen ə'meɹɪkn ɪ'dɪʃn 'paɹɪətɪd frəm ði 'ɪŋglɪʃ pʊblɪ'keɪʃn æz əv 'kɒs ɔl ɪ'dɪʃnz 'wɜ hæd ə semɪ'hjumɹəs edɪ'tɔɹɪəl 'pɹefɪs 'daʊtɪŋ ðət ðə 'bʊk 'æktʃəli kʊd bi ðə pɹə'dɛkʃn əv ən 'ɪŋglɪʃ 'leɪdi. ði 'ɪŋglɪʃ 'leɪdɪz ə 'nɒt wɒt aɪ bɪ'liv ðəm tə 'bi ɪf ðeɪ ɔɹ 'eni wen əv ðəm wʊd sɜʊ 'fɑ fə'get 'wɒt wəz 'dju tə ðəm'selvz n ðə 'kæɹɪktəɹ əv ðeə 'kentɹi əz tʊ 'lend ðeə 'neɪm n 'sæŋkʃn tu ə 'gɹɜʊs vaə'leɪʃn əv ðə 'kɒmən dɪ'kɔɹəmz əv 'laɪf. 'ðæt 'edɪtə wəz 'ɹaɪtɪŋ wɪð 'tɐŋ ɪn 'tʃik 'beɪsɪkli bət ðeə wə 'θaʊznz hu 'ɛkoʊd ðə 'sentɪmənt 'kwaɪt 'sɪɹɪəsli. 'mɪsɪs 'tɪɒləp wɒt ə 'neɪm! ɪn ɪt'self ən əfens! 'kʊd ɪt bi 'tɹu? hu'evə ʃi 'wɒz wəz 'sɜtənli 'nɜʊ 'leɪdi.

EXERCISE
1:10
# GA Phonetic Transcription

Transcribe the following passage into normal English orthography.

ʃi 'nɛvɚ 'tɹʌbld tə dʒʌstɪfaɪ hɚ 'steɪɾəs əz ə leɪdi tə ðɪ ə'mɛɹəknz. ʃi 'nɛvɚ dɪd 'mʌtʃ ə'palədʒaɪzɪŋ ɔɹ ɛks'pleɪnɪŋ al hɚ 'laɪf 'laŋ. 'niðɚ dɪd ʃi ɹemə'nɪs ə'baʊt hɚ 'laɪf ɪn aɹoʊbaɪ'agɹəfi ɔɹ 'mɛmwaɹz. ʍat wəz 'pæst wəz 'pæst tə 'fæni 'tɹaləp.

ʃi wəz 'bɔɹn an ðə 'tɛnθ əv 'maɹtʃ 'sɛvntin eɪɾi faɪv 'jiɹz 'leɪɾɚ ðən 'dʒeɪn 'astən hʊm ʃi 'nɛvɚ 'nu 'mɔɹz ðə 'pɪɾi sɪns ðeɪ 'boʊθ əb'zɝvd 'mænɚz wɪð ən aɪ'ɹanɪk aɪ. ʃi wəz ðə 'daɾɚ əv ðə 'ɹevɹnd 'wɪljəm 'mɪlʔn n hɪz 'waɪf hu wɚ 'lɪvɪŋ ət ðə 'taɪm ɪn ðə 'vɪlədʒ əv 'steɪplɪn 'niɹ 'bɹɪstəl. ðeɪ kɹɪsnd hɚ ðeɪ 'sɛknd daɾɚ wɪð ə 'neɪm soʊ 'papjələ dʊɹɪŋ ðoʊz 'jiɹz ðəɾ ɪt 'simz 'hæf ðə 'gɝl 'tʃɪldɹn əv 'ɪŋlənd ɪn ðə 'læst əv ðɪ 'eɪɾinθ m bə'gɪnɪŋ əv ðə 'naɪntinθ 'sɛntʃɹi wɚ 'neɪmd 'frænsəs ŋ 'kald 'fæni.

'sun 'æftɚ hɚ 'bɝθ ðə 'ɹevɹnd 'mɪlʔn wəz ə'wɔɹdɪd ðə 'lɪvɪŋ ət 'hɛkfild ɪn 'nɔɹθ 'hæmpʃɚ n 'sɪksti 'maɪlz fɹəm 'lʌndn. ə 'jiɹ ɔɹ soʊ 'leɪɾɚ ə 'sʌn 'hæri wəz 'bɔɹn n 'fɔɹtli ðɛ'ɹæftɚ ðə 'mʌðɚ əv 'meɹi 'fɹænsəs n 'hɛnɹi 'daɪd.

EXERCISE
1:11
# Transcription from Orthography to Phonetics

Render the following sentences (i) in a broad phonetic transcription and (ii) into a narrow transcription of your own casual pronunciation. We suggest that you record yourself (or, alternatively, a friend with a similar accent) saying the sentences at a normal speech rate and attempt to write down exactly what you hear when you play back the tape. Say what accent you are transcribing.

a.  Did you happen to see my brother on your way here today?
b.  What are you going to do when you graduate?
c.  Are you likely to eat all that pasta on your plate?
d.  It's a lot later than I thought it was and we have to catch a train for London.
e.  This is the story of the different ways we looked for treasure, and I think when you read it you will see that we were not lazy about the looking.
f.  The mole had been working hard all morning spring-cleaning his little home.

Compare your two transcriptions, commenting on the differences between the broad and the narrow renderings.

# EXERCISE 1:12   Nonsense Words

Read out the following nonsense words. Say which of them could be words of English and which could not (intermediate judgements are possible).

| | | | | |
|---|---|---|---|---|
| [slubal] | [tsiɹtɪk] | [aɹblu] | [apik] | [prouto] |
| [ftik] | [qako] | [keɪg] | [mɛkət] | [gnaugɔl] |
| [ptɒmtɪk] | [duluke] | [ɔzɪbɪlɪn] | [ɹaɪk] | [ŋægæ] |
| [æŋæŋ] | [huʎæk] | [pɹehɪp] | [ɚtaka] | [ɝtaka] |
| [kwækou] | [ʌpɐlə] | [zɔɪhap] | [ʃau] | [ʧɪnʤ] |
| [ʃɹɪʒu] | [ʒɯgɯ] | [ifʉkʉlə] | [dɹul] | [ðɛʒɔʔ] |
| [ʔɨpɐg] | [θɛʒɔʔ] | [dʌ] | [dʊt] | [dɐt] |
| [tyt] | [bœd] | [ødø] | [ʧiɣɐ] | [xaɦa] |

# EXERCISE 1:13   GA Phonetic Transcription

The following passage has no word breaks or stressed syllables marked. Transcribe it into normal English orthography, including word breaks and punctuation.

gɹeɪtsɹɹizɚbɔɹnnatmeɪdðəbɪldɪŋzwɪdəlaɹɹɪndəskwɛɹzmpaɹksðətgɪvʌzsoumʌʧpleʒɚɚn atðəpɹadʌktəvtaunplænɪŋsouʃkanʃnsɔɹivngudbɪznəsðəmanjuməntsnspeɪsəswɪɹətɝntuɹ ndeɪlaɪtnɪndɹiɪmzɚðɪʌnlaɪkliafspɹɪŋəvsɪvəlaɪzeɪʃnzmoustekstætɪkroumænsðəgɹændjun jənəvmʌninvænəɹi

# EXERCISE 1:14   RP Phonetic Transcription

The following passage has no word breaks or stressed syllables marked. Transcribe it into normal English orthography, including word breaks and punctuation.

mɐninvænətibɪltwestmɪnstəɹæbinsmpɔlzkəθidɹəlleɪdauthaɪdpakswɔmdɐpðɪaɪfltauəɹɹe ɪzdðəhelmzlindəkraɪzləbɪldɪŋzwɒthəvðətɛɹəsɪzəvnæʃɔʤəsplendəzəvbauhaustəduwɪðnəs esətiɪtɪzɝtənðətwɪnidbɪldɪŋznðətɪnsemgreɪtsɪtizlaɪknjujɔkðʒuzbɪldɪŋzməstgɝʊɐpwədz

# EXERCISE Faulty Transcription
## 1:15

The transcription of the passage below is riddled with errors. You should identify these errors, correct them, and then transcribe the passage into normal orthography.

ɪn ðiːz lɛktʃəz aɪ wəd laɪk tʊ ɛksplɔɹ ə nʌmbəɹ əf ɪʃuz ɹɪlatɪŋ tə hjumən cɔgnətɪv kəpæsɪtɪz n ðə mɛntəl stɹʌctʃəs ðət sɜv əz viəklz fə ðɪ ɛksəcaɪz əv thɪz kapæsətɪz. pleɪnli ðɪs fɔmjuleɪʃn əv ə pɹobləm ɛmbɒdɪz assʌmʃnz ðət ə fɑ fɹəm klɪə ənd ə haɪli cɒntɹəvɜʃl ɪnsoʊfaɹ əz ðeɪ ɑ klɪə. aɪ wɪll traɪ tə meɪk ðəm klɪəɹə ænd aɪ hoʊp mɔ plɔzɪbl əz aɪ pɹəsɪd. ɪn ðɪ ɛnd ðə bɛst weɪ tə klæɹɪfaɪ ðɪz asʌmpʃnz ənd tʊ ɪvæljuate ðəm ɪz tə kənstɹʌkt spəsɪfik mɔdlz gaɪdɪd baɪ ðəm ɪn pətɪkjʊlar dəmeɪnz ðɛn to ask haʊ ðɪz mɒdlz feə wɛn ɪntəpɹətɪd əz ɛxplænətɹi θiəɹɪz. ɪf ðə lidɪŋ aɪdɪəz əɹ əppɹoʊpɹɪət ðeɪ wɪl bɪ ʃapənd ən jʌstɪfaɪd baɪ thə sʌksɛs əv ɛksplænətri ðiəɹɪz θət dɪvɛləp ðəm ɪn ə spəsɪfik weɪ. aɪ wɪl nɒt atɛmpt ə systəmatɪk prɛzənteɪʃn əv sʌch ə mɒdl hɪə bət wɪl dɪskʌs pɹɒpətɪz əv som ðət ə bɪŋg ɪnvɛstɪgeɪtɪd ðoʊ ɪn tɛchnɪkl stʌdɪz ðeɪ ə nɒt pɹɛzɛntɪd ɪn ðɪz termz wɪtʃ aɪ wɒnt tə sʌggɛst ə ðɪ əpɹoʊpɹɪət tɜmz. ðə kɒgnɪtɪv dəmeɪn ðət wɪl pɹɪmeɹili kənsɜn mi ɪz humən læŋgwɪʤ. ðə ɹizn fə ðə tʃɔɪs ɪz ɪn pat pɜsnl ɹɪlatɪŋ tə lɪmɪts əv maɪ oʊn ʌnderstændɪŋ. aɪ θɪnk ɪt feə tə seɪ hoʊɛvə ðət ðɪ ɪʃuz ə mɔɹ izɪli formjuleɪtɪd əm bɛtə undəstood ɪn kənɛktʃn wɪð hjumən læŋgwɪʤ thæn ʌðə dəmeɪnz əv hjumən kɒgnɪʃn – wɪtʃ ɪz nɒt tə seɪ ðət theɪ ɑ klɪəli fɔmjuleɪtɪd ɔ wɛl ʌndəstud. ðeɪ ɑ sʌm hu wʊd vɜtʃəli aɪdɛntɪfaɪ ðə stʌdi əv læŋguɪʤ n ðə stʌdi ov maɪnd kwaɪn fəɹ ɛgzɑmple. ðɪs ɪz nɒt maɪ own vju.

# II

# Foundations of Phonology

The existence of phonology is justified by the fact that, in any particular language, speech sounds do not pattern randomly. Each language has its own system of sound oppositions, expressed as phonemes. Phonemes can undergo contextual determination and split into a number of allophones. In generative phonology, sound oppositions are ascribed, not to the surface, as they are in Saussure-inspired phonology, but to an abstract underlying level of representation, related to the phonetic level of actual sound by means of a set of phonological rules. Each phonological rule carries out a change in the input representation. The joint action of the rules makes up a derivation, the output of which provides the phonetic representation of the surface form. The primitive building blocks of the sound system are, however, neither phonemes nor underlying segments, but, rather, distinctive features. A bundle of distinctive features, each specified for a particular value, usually + (plus) or − (minus), defines a segment. Overlap between segments in feature specification is taken as the expression of a natural class, formalizable by a common distinctive feature or features. Neighbouring segments tend to share feature specifications, a target frequently driving assimilation, whether partial or total. Word-bounded harmony, usually affecting vowels, instantiates a particularly strong type of assimilation. Local vowel harmony is commonly referred to as "umlaut". In the autosegmental mode of representation, each feature occupies its own autonomous layer, or "tier", and is linked to other features by means of association lines. This type of configuration conveniently constrains the mutual interaction of features in rules. Some feature tiers are universally dependent on other feature tiers. The hierarchical edifice of features ultimately rests on the timing tier, or skeleton, abstractly responsible for both the linear arrangement and the temporal organization of speech sounds. The timing tier provides a formal tool for the principled separation of the qualitative and the quantitative aspects of segments.

**Japanese**
## 2:1

a.   In Japanese the sounds [s] and [ʃ] are in complementary distribution.

|          |                    |
|----------|--------------------|
| [kesa]   | 'this morning'     |
| [aʃita]  | 'tomorrow'         |
| [osoi]   | 'slow, late'       |
| [ʃimasu] | '(I will) do (it)' |
| [kusaru] | 'to rot'           |
| [muʃi]   | 'insect'           |
| [ase]    | 'sweat'            |
| [miso]   | 'soy bean paste'   |
| [toʃi]   | 'year'             |

(i)   Give an account of this distribution using phonetic symbols.

(ii)  Assuming one of these two complementary sounds ([s] or [ʃ]) to be the lexical representation, which of the two sounds is derived?

(iii) Write a rule with phonetic symbols to derive the phonetic form from the lexical one.

b.   The following data, also from Japanese, show the complementary distribution of [t] and [ʧ].

|           |               |
|-----------|---------------|
| [tatari]  | 'curse'       |
| [ʧikaku]  | 'near'        |
| [ita]     | 'board'       |
| [keʧi]    | 'stingy'      |
| [satori]  | 'realization' |
| [otoko]   | 'man'         |
| [moʧi]    | 'rice cake'   |
| [uʧi]     | 'house'       |

(iv)  Give an account of the distribution of [t] and [ʧ] and make a suggestion about the lexical form.

(v)   How are the distributional facts in (a) and (b) related?

# EXERCISE 2:2 German Obstruents

In chapter 2 of *A Course in Phonology* we explain that lexical forms are those which are listed in the lexicon and effectively have to be learned. The phonetic representation, on the other hand, can be predicted by rule. Consider the distribution of German obstruents from the following set of data. (NB: the final orthographic *e* corresponds to phonetic schwa in German.)

a.

| | |
|---|---|
| Ta[k] | 'day' |
| Rau[p] | 'robbery' |
| lei[t] | 'sorry' |
| Lo[p] | 'praise' |
| We[k] | 'way' |
| Lan[t] | 'land' |
| Grei[s] | 'old man' |
| bra[f] | 'obedient' (pred.) |
| Ra[t] | 'advice' |
| Vol[k] | 'people' |
| Perisko[p] | 'periscope' |
| Ho[f] | 'courtyard' |
| Ro[s] | 'horse' |

b.

| | |
|---|---|
| Ta[g]e | 'days' |
| rau[b]en | 'to rob' |
| lei[d]en | 'to suffer' |
| lo[b]en | 'to praise' |
| We[g]e | 'ways' |
| lan[d]en | 'to land' |
| Grei[z]es | 'old men' |
| bra[v]er | 'obedient' (masc.) |
| ra[t]en | 'to advise' |
| Vol[k]e | 'peoples' |
| Perisko[p]e | 'periscopes' |
| Hö[f]e | 'courtyards' |
| Ro[s]e | 'horses' |

(i) What is the lexical form of the alternating obstruents in the data, and why?

(ii) Account for the difference between the lexical and phonetic forms.

(iii) Give a rule to derive the phonetic forms from the lexical forms.

# EXERCISE 2:3  Dutch Past Tense Suffix

In chapter 2 of *A Course in Phonology* we introduce three different cases of regressive (right to left) assimilation in English. Two of these involved the assimilation of place of articulation of one segment to that of the following sound, and the other the devoicing of voiced fricatives when the following sound is voiceless. Clearly, assimilatory processes could in principle work in either direction. When the conditioning sound precedes the affected one (left to right) we call the process *progressive* assimilation.

The past tense suffix for regular verbs in Dutch is either /tə/ or /də/ (the italicized forms are in standard Dutch orthography: we ignore vowel length in the transcriptions).

a.  | *klapte* | [klɑptə] | 'applauded' |
    | *krabde* | [krɑbdə] | 'scratched' |
    | *redde* | [rɛdə] | 'saved' |
    | *viste* | [vɪstə] | 'fished' |
    | *raasde* | [razdə] | 'raged' |
    | *zette* | [zɛtə] | 'put' |
    | *mafte* | [mɑftə] | 'slept' |
    | *kloofde* | [klovdə] | 'split' |
    | *legde* | [lɛɣdə] | 'laid' |
    | *lachte* | [lɑxtə] | 'laughed' |

(i)    What determines which form of the suffix will be attached to the stem?

(ii)   What sort of process is illustrated in these data?

(iii)  Is it possible, from the data supplied above, to determine the lexical representation of the suffix?

(iv)   The forms [zɛtə] and [rɛdə] would appear to be counterexamples to any rule you might postulate. Can you explain why, in fact, they are not? What else is going on here?

Now reconsider (iii) in the light of the further data supplied in (b).

b.  | *roemde* | [rumdə] | 'praised' |
    | *zoende* | [zundə] | 'kissed' |
    | *mengde* | [mɛŋdə] | 'mixed' |
    | *roerde* | [rurdə] | 'stirred' |
    | *rolde* | [rɔldə] | 'rolled' |
    | *aaide* | [ajdə] | 'caressed' |
    | *skiede* | [skidə] | 'skied' |

EXERCISE **Yiddish**
2:4

Yiddish is a Germanic language which exhibits many similarities to German (see exercise 2:2). However, if you consider the data in the left columns of (a) and (b) below, you will see that there is one significant way in which the two languages differ. What is this? (The data in (a) show a process which occurs in all speech styles, whereas the process represented in (b) is a casual speech phenomenon.)

a.  [ʃraib]        '(I) write'          [ʃraipst]         '(you (sing.)) write'
    [red]          '(I) speak'          [retst]           '(you (sing.)) speak'
    [vog]          'weight'             [vokʃol]          'scales'
    [briv]         'letter'             [briftregər]      'postman'
    [aiz]          'ice'                [aiskastn]        'ice box'
    [ʃantaʒ]       'blackmail'          [ʃantaʃ ʃtik]     'blackmailing tactics'

b.  [uf]           'up'                 [uvvekn]          'wake up'
    [bux]          'book'               [buɣgeʃeft]       'bookshop'
    [bak]          'cheek'              [bagbein]         'cheekbone'
    [kop]          'head'               [kobveitik]       'headache'
    [zis]          'sweet'              [zizvarg]         'sweets' (confectionery)
    [ra(ə)ʃ]       'noise'              [ra(ə)ʒdik]       'noisy'
    [vait]         'far'                [vaidzeəvdik]     'farsighted'
    [ʃvits]        'sweat'              [ʃvidzbod]        'steambath'

(i)    Describe the processes operating in (a) and (b).

(ii)   In what way do the two cases differ?

(iii)  Suggest what the lexical forms of the words represented in both sets of data might be.

(iv)   Write a rule which will derive the phonetic forms from the lexical forms.

# EXERCISE 2:5   Spanish

Consider the following examples of the pre-consonantal distribution of nasals and laterals in Spanish:

| | | | |
|---|---|---|---|
| u[m][p]ie | 'a foot' | e[l̪][d̪]ueño | 'the owner' |
| a[l̪t̪]o | 'high' | e[nl]ace | 'link' |
| sa[lb]o | 'safe' | e[mb]iar | 'to send' |
| a[n̪t̪]es | 'before' | sue[l̪d̪]o | 'salary' |
| co[ʎtʃ]a | 'bedspread' | si[ɲ][ʎ]egar | 'without arriving' |
| ci[ŋk]o | 'five' | ni[ŋg]uno | 'nobody' |
| á[ŋx]el | 'angel' | sa[ls]a | 'sauce' |
| o[n̪θ]e | 'eleven' | si[n̪θ]ero | 'sincere' |
| e[mp]ezar | 'to begin' | a[lg]uno | 'some' |
| e[ns]ayo | 'test' | co[n̪d̪]e | 'earl' |
| e[l̪][t̪]oro | 'the bull' | u[m][b]astón | 'a stick' |
| e[l̪][θ]ielo | 'the sky' | a[l̪θ]ar | 'to lift' |
| pla[ɲtʃ]ar | 'to iron' | e[ʎ][ʎ]ano | 'the plain' |
| u[n][n]iño | 'a boy' | e[l][n]iño | 'the boy' |
| e[l][b]astón | 'the stick' | e[l][x]erez | 'the sherry' |

(i)   List the various manifestations of the lateral and nasal consonants in the data set.

(ii)   Describe the distribution of each variant.

(iii)   Do you detect a difference in the behaviour of nasals and laterals? What motivates this difference?

(iv)   Write the appropriate rules to account for the distribution of the nasal consonants and the lateral consonants.

# EXERCISE 2:6 **Kannada Prefixation**

Kannada is a Dravidian language spoken in Southern India. Analyse the following data. (NB: *h* is historically derived from *p*; = indicates a compound boundary.)

| | | | |
|---|---|---|---|
| kaṇṇu | 'eye' | keŋgaṇṇu | 'red eye' |
| taḷir | 'sprout' | kendaḷir | 'red sprout' |
| hallu | 'tooth' | kembal | 'red tooth' |
| kiraṇa | 'rays' | keŋgiraṇa | 'red rays' |
| tsiguru | 'sprout' | kendʑiguru | 'red sprout' |
| tale | 'head' | kendale | 'red head' |
| na=lige | 'tongue' | kenna=lige | 'red tongue' |
| mugilu | 'sky' | kemmugilu | 'red sky' |
| tere | 'screen' | heddere | 'big screen' |
| handi | 'pig' | hebbandi | 'big pig' |
| kumbaḷa | 'pumpkin' | heggumbaḷa | 'big pumpkin' |
| dʑe=nu | 'bee' | hedʑdʑe=nu | 'big bee' |
| mara | 'tree' | hemmara | 'big tree' |

Hints: Bear in mind that phonology is autosegmental and that segments can have partially specified representations.

(i)     What is the lexical form of the prefix which translates as 'red'?

(ii)    How does it acquire its surface form? Write the appropriate rule(s).

(iii)   What is the lexical form of the prefix which translates as 'big'?

(iv)   How does it acquire its surface form? Give the appropriate rule(s).

(v)    Account for the voice alternations in the initial consonant of the nouns.

(vi)   Give the Kannada for 'red pig', 'red bee', 'big head' and 'big sky'.

# EXERCISE 2:7 Akan Vowel Harmony

Akan has the vowel system displayed in the following two sets.

|   |   |   |   |
|---|---|---|---|
| i | u | ɪ | ʊ |
| e | o | ɛ | ɔ |
|   | a |   |   |

(i)    Work out the distinctive feature specifications of this vowel system. What is the feature which distinguishes the two sets?

Akan words display vowel harmony, as the examples in (a) show:

a.    o-fiti-i        'he pierced it'
      ɔ-cɪrɛ-ɪ       'he showed it'
      e-bu-o        'nest'
      ɛ-bʊ-ɔ        'stone'
      ɔ-bɛ-jɛ-ɪ      'he came and did it'
      o-be-ji-i       'he came and removed it'

(ii)   Show how the harmony process works.

(iii)  Is the process directional?

In (b) we list some apparently non-harmonic forms:

b.    o-bisa-ɪ       'he asked it'
      ɔ-kari-i        'he weighed it'
      pɪrako         'pig'
      fuɲanɪ         'to search'

(iv)   What is the factor common to all these non-harmonic forms?

(v)    Making full use of the autosegmental machinery available, account for the forms in (a) and those in (b).

Finally, consider the form o-ɲanɪ 'he has woken up' (*cf*. ɲanɪ 'to wake up')

(vi)   Can this form be integrated into the account you have given for (a) and (b)?

# EXERCISE 2:8 Tahltan Coronals

Tahltan is an Athapaskan language spoken in British Columbia. The set of data in (a) shows the phonetic variation exhibited by the first person singular morpheme and that in (b) the variation in the first person dual marker. (NB: the superscript ' denotes an ejective articulation, although this is irrelevant to the exercise.)

a.  First person singular

| | | |
|---|---|---|
| /θɛ+s+ðɛɬ/ | → [θɛθðɛɬ] | 'I'm hot' |
| /hudi+s+ʧa/ | → [hudiʃʧa] | 'I love them' |
| /ɛ+s+k'a/ | → [ɛsk'a] | 'I'm gutting fish' |
| /dɛ+s+kʷʊθ/ | → [dɛθkʷʊθ] | 'I cough' |
| /ɛ+s+duːθ/ | → [ɛθduːθ] | 'I whipped him' |
| /ɛ+s+ʤini/ | → [ɛʃʤini] | 'I'm singing' |
| /nadɛdɛː+s+baːtɬ/ | → [nadɛdɛːsbaːtɬ] | 'I hung myself' |
| /ta+s+tθaɬ/ | → [taθtθaɬ] | 'I'm dying' |
| /ɬɛnɛ+s+ʧuːʃ/ | → [ɬɛnɛʃʧuːʃ] | 'I'm folding it' |
| /ɛ+s+dan/ | → [ɛsdan] | 'I'm drinking' |

(i)   Which sounds trigger the changes in the first person singular marker?

(ii)  Work out which distinctive features are common to the triggering sounds.

(iii) Write a rule to account for the facts that you have observed.

In (b) we show a similar process applying to the first person dual morpheme.

b.  First person dual

| | |
|---|---|
| [dɛθigɪtɬ] | 'we two threw it' |
| [dɛsidzɛl] | 'we two shouted' |
| [naθibaːtɬ] | 'we two hung it' |
| [iʃiʧotɬ] | 'we two blew it up' |
| [uʃidʒɛ] | 'we two are called' |
| [xasiːdets] | 'we two plucked it' |
| [nisit'aːts] | 'we two got up' |
| [dɛsit'ʌs] | 'we two are walking' |
| [tɛɛdɛnɛʃidʒuːt] | 'we two chased it away' |

(iv)  Based on the observations you made from the data in (a), can you suggest what the underlying form of the first person dual marker is?

# EXERCISE 2:9 Japanese Again

In Japanese the sounds [ç], [h] and [ɸ] are in complementary distribution (upper-case N represents a syllable final nasal whose ultimate place of articulation is determined by the following sound, if there is one, or else is pronounced uvular):

a.   [joho:]      'forecast'
     [to:ɸu]      'tofu'
     [ɸuku]       'clothes'
     [hoʃi]       'star'
     [çito]       'person'
     [ko:çi:]     'coffee'
     [heN]        'strange'
     [hako]       'box'
     [tehoN]      'model'
     [ɸukai]      'deep'
     [saiɸu]      'wallet'
     [ku:çi]      'waste'
     [ʃihai]      'control'
     [eɸu]        'F'
     [kiçin]      'grace'

(i)    State the distribution of these three sounds.

(ii)   Is it possible to say which of the three alternants is underlying and which are derived? If so, what is the answer?

(iii)  How can distinctive feature theory explain this distribution?

(iv)   Write appropriate autosegmental rules to account for this distribution.

# EXERCISE 2:10 **Eastern Cheremis**

In the Finno-Volgaic language Eastern Cheremis, spoken in Russia, certain suffixes exhibit the harmonic alternation we show in (a) and (b):

a. 
|  |  |
|---|---|
| kit-ʃe | 'his hand' |
| surt-ʃo | 'his house' |
| ergə-ʒe | 'his boy' |
| yp-ʃø | 'his hair' |
| kobaʃtə-ʒe | 'its fur' |
| pørtəʃtə-ʒø | 'in his house' |
| boz-ʒo | 'his wagon' |
| ʃuʒar-ʒe | 'his sister' |

b. 
|  |  |
|---|---|
| ʧodra-ʃte | 'forest' (inessive) |
| pørtə-ʃtø | 'house' (inessive) |
| budʑə-ʃto | 'head' (inessive) |
| leʃ-ne | 'near' |
| myndər-nø | 'in the distance' |
| pur-mo | 'entering' |

(i)   List the vowels of Eastern Cheremis, together with their feature specifications.

(ii)   Which vowels trigger the harmony process?

(iii)   Which features spread?

(iv)   What is the lexical specification of the vowel in the suffix in (a)?

(v)   Show how it acquires its full specification.

(vi)   What are the suffix vowels in the following words:

|  |  |
|---|---|
| bokten-ʒV | 'beside it' |
| kornə-ʒV | 'his way' |
| sør-ʒV | 'its milk' |

The first person plural suffix -na does not alternate:

c. 
|  |  |
|---|---|
| ʧodra-na | 'our forest' |
| pørt-na | 'our house' |
| budʑ-na | 'our head' |
| ergə-na | 'our son' |

(vii)   Explain why.

# EXERCISE 2:11 A Child's Language

The data listed below come from a child of around two years of age. They differ from his father's RP pronunciation in a number of ways. You should first transcribe the adult forms and then suggest what the specific differences are. Finally, write a set of rules to describe the changes that the child makes. There are a number of homophones in the data; the rules you write should predict this. (All except one of the differences concern consonants.)

| | | | |
|---|---|---|---|
| [maɪt] | mice | [bɑk] | park |
| [naɪt] | nice | [bɛk] | peg |
| [dut] | juice | [beɪ] | play |
| [dɒn] | John | [bu] | blue |
| [deɪdi] | lazy | [bu] | blow |
| [deɪdi] | lady | [ɛbu] | elbow |
| [gʌm] | come | [gɑk] | dark |
| [gɔnə] | corner | [gɪk] | drink |
| [maɪp] | knife | [gɒk] | sock |
| [ŋeɪk] | snake | [gʌk] | duck |
| [daɪt] | light | [gɒk] | lock |
| [gaɪk] | like | [gi] | key |
| [gɪk] | kiss | [gɒk] | cloth |

Hint: there are eight different processes operating in this sample.

# EXERCISE 2:12 Zoque

Consider the examples below of nasal prefixation of obstruent-initial stems in Zoque (a language of Mexico):

| | | | | |
|---|---|---|---|---|
| a. | pama | 'clothing' | mbama | 'my clothing' |
| | tatah | 'father' | ndatah | 'my father' |
| | kwarto | 'room' | ŋgwarto | 'my room' |
| | plato | 'plate' | mblato | 'my plate' |
| | trama | 'trap' | ndrama | 'my trap' |
| | disko | 'record' | ndisko | 'my record' |
| | gaju | 'rooster' | ŋgaju | 'my rooster' |

| ʧoʔngoja | 'rabbit' | ɲʤoʔngoja | 'my rabbit' |
| tsima | 'calabash' | nʤima | 'my calabash' |
| sʌk | 'beans' | sʌk | 'my beans' |
| faha | 'belt' | faha | 'my belt' |
| ʃapun | 'soap' | ʃapun | 'my soap' |

(i)   What effect has nasal prefixation on the stem initial obstruent?

(ii)  What effect does a stem-initial fricative have on nasal prefixation? What do the data tell us about affricates?

(iii) What happens to the nasal prefix otherwise?

(iv)  Formalize the processes by means of rules.

# EXERCISE **Kutep**
# 2:13

The phonetic inventory of the West African language Kutep includes a number of labialized consonants. Examples of words containing these are shown below ([ɕ] is a voiceless prepalatal fricative and [ʑ] is its voiced equivalent; [t͡ɕ] is, of course, a prepalatal affricate; the accents on some of the vowels represent tones, which may be ignored).

| bapʷà | 'they grind' |
| batʷáp | 'they picked up' |
| bat͡sˤáp | 'they chose' |
| bat͡ɕˤák | 'they sleep' |
| nsázᵛakkʷà | 'the water is hot' |
| babʷa | 'they deceived' |
| bambʷà | 'they tasted' |
| bandʷap | 'they wove' |
| baŋgʷà | 'they drink' |
| bamʷà | 'they measured' |
| baŋʷáŋ | 'they slip' |
| basˤa | 'they kneel' |
| baskʷáp | 'they are foolish' |
| aɕˤápaŋ | 'groundnuts' |
| baʑᵛam | 'they begged' |

(i)   In what way do these data confirm those from Zoque in the previous exercise?

(ii)  What is the factor responsible for the phonetic form of the labialized element?

# EXERCISE 2:14 Slovak Vowel Length

Slovak contrasts long and short syllable nuclei at the lexical and phonetic levels, as we show in the examples in (a):

a.  krik     'shout'     kriːk     'bush'
    kura     'chicken'     kuːra     'cure'
    rad     'row'     graːd     'degree'

In addition, the language has morphologically conditioned vowel lengthening, as we can see in the examples in (b):

b.  *Nom. sg.*     *Gen. pl.*
    piv+ɔ     piːv     'beer'
    put+ɔ     puːt     'chain'
    lan+ɔ     laːn     'cable'

    znak     'sign'     znaːʧ+ik     'sign' (dim.)
    puk     'bud'     puːʧ+ik     'bud' (dim.)

In the cases exemplified in (c), the alternation manifests as diphthongization:

c.  *Nom. sg.*     *Gen. pl.*
    ʧɛl+ɔ     ʧiɛl     'forehead'
    kɔl+ɔ     kuɔl     'wheel'
    mæs+ɔ     mias     'meat'

    ʧlovɛk     'man'     ʧloviɛʧ+ik     'man' (dim.)
    krɔk     'step'     kruɔʧ+ik     'step' (dim.)

(i)     List the vowels that undergo the alternations in (b) and in (c).

(ii)     Making use of the separation of the skeletal tier and the melody tier, write rules to derive the genitive plurals in (b) and (c).

Many Slovak suffixes are subject to a "Rhythmic Law", as illustrated in (d):

d.  *Neuter nouns*

| *Nom. sg.* | *Nom. pl.* | *Dat. pl.* | *Loc. pl.* | |
|---|---|---|---|---|
| lan+ɔ | lan+aː | lan+aːm | lan+aːch | 'cable' |
| staːd+ɔ | staːd+a | staːd+am | staːd+ach | 'herd' |
| ʧiːsl+ɔ | ʧiːsl+a | ʧiːsl+am | ʧiːsl+ach | 'number' |

*Agentive* -nik

| | | |
|---|---|---|
| hut+a | hut+niːk | 'steel works' |
| mɔntaːʒ | mɔntaːʒ+nik | 'assembling' |
| ʧaluːn | ʧaluːn+nik | 'wallpaper' |

(iii) Show how the alternation between the long and short vowels works.

(iv) Provide a formal account of the alternation.

The Rhythmic Law also applies when the stem contains a diphthong:

e.

| *Nom. sg.* | *Nom. pl.* | *Dat. pl.* | *Loc. pl.* | |
|---|---|---|---|---|
| miɛst+ɔ | miɛst+a | miɛst+am | miɛst+ach | 'place' |
| hniɛzd+ɔ | hniɛzd+a | hniɛzd+am | hniɛzd+ach | 'nest' |

*Agentive* -nik

| | | |
|---|---|---|
| papiɛr | papiɛr+nik | 'paper' |
| pɔʒiar | pɔʒiar+nik | 'fire' |

| | |
|---|---|
| strɛʒ+iɛ+m | 'I guard' |
| muɔʒ+ɛ+m | 'I can' |

(v) Show how the Rhythmic Law and the diphthongization process give the correct output in the following words:

ʧiːsl+a
miɛst+am
strɛʒ+iɛ+m
muɔʒ+ɛ+m

# III

# Syllables

Many facts of language which appear capricious at first sight become well motiv-ated when we postulate a suprasegmental, or "prosodic", structure organizing segments in certain ways. We refer to such clusters of segments as "syllables". Segments possess different degrees of a property known as "sonority", essentially correlating with amount of sound. Each syllable can usefully be construed as a sonority mountain, in which a nucleus (usually a vowel), attracts segments of lower sonority on either side. The core syllable is made up of a consonant and a vowel (CV), constituting respectively the onset and the nucleus of the syllable. Such core syllables are the first acquired by children, and are present in all of the languages of the world. Syllable complexity can be achieved by the incorporation of a coda (a consonant after the nucleus: CVC) or incrementing the number of segments in any one subconstituent (CCV, CVV, etc.). The nucleus and the coda group together in a subconstituent "rime", which pairs with the onset to make up the syllable. The profile of the syllable is by definition subject to Sonority Sequencing, that is, to the principle that sonority climbs up until it peaks, and then climbs down. Moreover, construction of onsets takes priority over construction of codas, at least minimally. Also, members of a same subconstituent may be required to be separated by a min-imum of sonority, specified language by language. Formally, syllables are anchored in the skeletal slots that constitute the baseline for the hierarchy of features. Untypically, but not infrequently, (high) vowels are allowed in the margins of syl-lables, and consonants (usually sonorant) in the nucleus. Some languages exhibit consonant clusters that violate Sonority Sequencing, or which are inordinately long, particularly at word edges: situations such as these pose an obvious challenge to the more constrained theories of the syllable.

**A French Language Game**

Consider the following sample of the language game *Verlan* (from *l'envers*, 'the wrong side'):

|   |   | French | Verlan |   |
|---|---|--------|--------|---|
| a. | gamin | [gamɛ̃] | [mɛ̃ga] | 'kid' (masc.) |
|   | gamine | [gamin] | [minga] | 'kid' (fem.) |
|   | copain | [kopɛ̃] | [pɛ̃ko] | 'mate' (masc.) |
|   | copine | [kopin] | [pinko] | 'mate' (fem.) |
|   | français | [frãsɛ] | [sɛfrã] | 'French' (masc.) |
|   | française | [frãsɛz] | [sɛzfrã] | 'French' (fem.) |
|   | fumer | [fyme] | [mefy] | 'to smoke' |
|   | finir | [finir] | [nirfi] | 'to finish' |

(i) What are the rules of the game?

In longer words there is more than one pattern, of which we only provide one for each word:

|   |   | French | Verlan |   |   |
|---|---|--------|--------|---|---|
| b. | rigolo | [rigolo] | [logori] | [ ... ] | 'funny' |
|   | tabouret | [tabure] | [rebuta] | [ ... ] | 'stool' |
|   | papillon | [papijɔ̃] | [jɔ̃pipa] | [ ... ] | 'butterfly' |
| c. | cigarette | [sigarɛt] | [garɛtsi] | [ ... ] | 'cigarette' |
|   | corrida | [korida] | [ridako] | [ ... ] | 'bull fight' |
| d. | enculé | [ãkyle] | [leãky] | [ ... ] | 'sod' |
|   | dégueulasse | [degølas] | [lasdegø] | [ ... ] | 'disgusting' |
|   | karaté | [karate] | [tekara] | [ ... ] | 'karate' |

(ii) Fill in the remaining possible forms.

# EXERCISE 3:2   Lenakel Epenthesis

The Austronesian language Lenakel uses vowel epenthesis to break up unsyllabifiable CC clusters:

a.    *Word Initial*

| | | |
|---|---|---|
| /t-n-ak-ol/ | [tɨnágɔl] | 'you (sg.) will do it' |
| /t-r-ep-ol/ | [tɨrébɔl] | 'he will then do it' |
| /n-n-ol/ | [nínɔl] | 'you (sg.) have done it' |
| /r-n-ol/ | [rɨnɔl] | 'he has done it' |

b.    *Word Medial*

| | | |
|---|---|---|
| /kam-n-m̃an-n/ | [kàmnɨm̃ánɨn] | 'for her brother' |
| /əs-ət-pn-aan/ | [əsɨdbənán] | 'don't go up there' |
| /k-ar-pkom/ | [karbə́gɔm] | 'they are heavy' |

c.    *Word Final*

| | | |
|---|---|---|
| /əpk-əpk/ | [əbgə́bək] | 'to be pregnant' |
| /apn-apn/ | [abnábən] | 'free' |
| /ark-ark/ | [argárɨkʰ] | 'to growl' |
| /r-əm-əŋn/ | [rɨmə́ŋən] | 'he was afraid' |
| /n-əm-əpk/ | [nɨmə́bəkʰ] | 'you (sg.) took it' |

(i)    List the syllable types possible in Lenakel.

(ii)    In the context of the possible syllable of Lenakel, in the examples in (c) there are potentially two positions that the epenthetic vowel could be located: which is the one that does not occur?

# EXERCISE 3:3   German Again

In Exercise 2:2 you formed a hypothesis about the distribution of obstruents in German. We repeat that data in (a) to remind you.

a.
| Ta[k] | 'day' | | b. | Ta[g]e | 'days' |
|---|---|---|---|---|---|
| Rau[p] | 'robbery' | | | rau[b]en | 'to rob' |
| lei[t] | 'sorry' | | | lei[d]en | 'to suffer' |
| Lo[p] | 'praise' | | | lo[b]en | 'to praise' |
| We[k] | 'way' | | | We[g]e | 'ways' |
| Lan[t] | 'land' | | | lan[d]en | 'to land' |
| Grei[s] | 'old man' | | | Grei[z]es | 'old men' |
| bra[f] | 'obedient' (pred.) | | | bra[v]er | 'obedient' (masc.) |
| Ra[t] | 'advice' | | | ra[t]en | 'to advise' |
| Vol[k] | 'people' | | | Vol[k]e | 'peoples' |
| Perisko[p] | 'periscope' | | | Perisko[p]e | 'periscopes' |
| Ho[f] | 'courtyard' | | | Hö[f]e | 'courtyards' |
| Ro[s] | 'horse' | | | Ro[s]e | 'horses' |

Now consider the further data set from German in (b). (NB: the vowel alternations are the result of the umlaut which we discuss in chapter 6 of *A Course in Phonology*):

| regsam | [rɛksam] | 'active' |
|---|---|---|
| Regung | [regʊŋ] | 'motion' |
| sagen | [zaːgən] | 'to say' |
| sagte | [zaːktə] | 'said' |
| Rad | [raːt] | 'wheel' |
| Räder | [rɛːdər] | 'wheels' |
| radfahren | [raːtfarən] | 'to cycle' |
| radeln | [raːdɛln] | 'to peddle' |
| staubig | [ʃtaʊbɪç] | 'dusty' |
| Stäubchen | [ʃtɔʏpçən] | 'dust particle' |
| stauben | [ʃtaʊbən] | 'to dust' |
| böse | [bøːzə] | 'wicked' |
| böshaft | [bøːshaft] | 'malicious' |
| braver | [braːvər] | 'obedient' |
| Bravheit | [braːfhaɪt] | 'good behaviour' |

Extend your earlier hypothesis to take this further information into account. Write the appropriate rule.

## EXERCISE Pali
## 3:4

Listed below are examples of consonant deletion and cluster simplification in Pali which occurred in the course of its historical evolution from its parent language Sanskrit.

|  | *Sanskrit* | *Pali* |  |
|---|---|---|---|
| a. | tatas | tato | 'therefrom' |
|  | punar | puno, puna | 'again' |
|  | praːpatat | papata | 'hurled down' |
| | | | |
| b. | danta | danta | 'tamed' |
|  | sambuddʰa | sambuddʰa | 'enlightened' |
|  | saktʰi | sattʰi | 'thigh' |
|  | mudga | mugga | 'bean' |
|  | śabda | sadda | 'words' |
|  | bʰakta | bʰatta | 'rice' |
|  | sapta | satta | 'seven' |
|  | karka | kakka | 'a precious stone' |
|  | sarpa | sappa | 'snake' |
|  | valka | vakka | 'the bark of a tree' |
|  | dʰarma | dʰamma | 'righteousness' |
|  | karṇa | kaṇṇa | 'ear' |
|  | kalmaṣa | kammasa | 'spotted' |
|  | karṣaka | kassaka | 'farmer' |
| | | | |
| c. | traana | taana | 'protection' |
|  | kramati | kamati | 'walks' |
|  | prati | paṭi | 'against' |
|  | śvaśru | sassu | 'mother-in-law' |

(i)   What do the data above tell you about the constraints on the possible syllable in Pali?

(ii)  What is the difference between the simplification of intervocalic clusters in (b) and that of word-initial clusters in (c).

(iii) Can this difference be traced back to syllable structure?

EXERCISE **English Vowel Deletion**
3:5

In fast speech in English (at least in our estimation) in unstressed word-initial syllables vowels may be deleted, sometimes creating what would normally be unacceptable onsets. In spite of this, there seem to be some restrictions on when a vowel may be deleted in seemingly similar situations. In (a) we list what we consider to be acceptable deletions and in (b) apparently similar words where deletion is not possible. Suggest what prevents deletion in the (b) cases. The relevant vowels are emboldened:

a.  *Deletion possible*
potato
syringe
career
commotion
phonetic
pathetic

b.  *No deletion possible*
reduction
retire
mature
promotion
laconic
platonic

EXERCISE **Icelandic**
3:6

Consider the following alternations from Icelandic, given in conventional Icelandic orthography (the orthographic symbol Þ is phonetically [θ]):

a.  | *Nominative sg.* | *Accusative sg.* | |
    | --- | --- | --- |
    | dag-ur | dag | 'day' |
    | stað-ur | stað | 'place' |
    | hest-ur | hest | 'horse' |
    | bæ-r | bæ | 'farmhouse' |
    | lækni-r | lækni | 'physician' |

b.  | | *Dative sg.* | |
    | --- | --- | --- |
    | lifur | lifri | 'liver' |
    | akur | agri | 'field' |
    | aldur | aldri | 'age' |

(i)     What are the variants of the nominative singular suffix?

(ii)    Do the data in (b) give you a clue as to the lexical form of this suffix?

Now consider the following data:

c.   

| Nom. sg. | Acc. sg. | Gen. sg. | Dat. pl. | Gen. pl. | |
|---|---|---|---|---|---|
| lyf-ur | lyf | lyf-s | lyfj-um | lyfj-a | 'medicine' |
| byl-ur | byl | byl-s | bylj-um | bylj-a | 'snowstorm' |
| söng-ur | söng | söng-s | söngv-um | söngv-a | 'song' |

(iii)   What in these examples helps to confirm your hypothesis as to the lexical form of the nominative singular suffix?

(iv)    What are the lexical forms of the genitive singular, genitive plural and dative plural suffixes?

(v)     Give a reason for the stem alternations observed in (c).

Consider the further data in (d):

d.   

| Nom. sg. | | Dat. pl. | | |
|---|---|---|---|---|
| barn | | börn-um | | 'child' |
| baggi | 'pack' | bögg-ull | | 'package' |
| jak-i | 'piece of ice' | jök-ul-l | | 'glacier' |
| Þagg-a | 'to silence' | Þög-ul-l | | 'taciturn' |
| kalla | 'call' (1st sg.) | köll-um | | 'call' (1st pl.) |

(vi)    Give a reason for the stem alternations in (d).

(vii)   In what way do the data in (e) below provide further evidence about the lexical form of the nominative suffix?

e.   

| akur | ökrum | 'field' |
|---|---|---|
| aldur | öldrum | 'age' |
| staður | stöðum | 'place' |

(viii)  Provide a formal account of all the alternations observed.

# EXERCISE 3:7 Anxiang Suffixation

The diminutive form in the Chinese language Anxiang is formed by the addition of the suffix -ər to a reduplicated form of the base. (Tones are omitted from the representations.)

| | | |
|---|---|---|
| tie | tie tiər | 'small dish, plate' |
| mian | mian miər | 'face' |
| tai | tai tər | 'belt' |
| pau | pau pər | 'bud' |
| ke | ke kər | 'check, chequer' |
| fa | fa fər | 'law, way' |
| o | o ər | 'bird's nest' |
| ti | ti tiər | 'bamboo flute' |
| tin | tin tiər | 'nail' |
| pʰu | pʰu pʰuər | 'spread' |
| tçy | tçy tçyər | 'pearl' |

Say which part of the base participates in the reduplicated forms, and why. (Hint: Anxiang is basically a monosyllabic language.)

# EXERCISE 3:8 Diola Fogny

In Diola Fogny, a Niger-Congo language spoken in Guinea-Bissau and Gambia, simplification occurs in cases where the concatenation of morphemes creates an unsyllabifiable consonant cluster, as we show in (a) (we have followed the transcription from the source; the symbol *j* represents a palatal obstruent and *y* represents [j]).

| a. | | | |
|---|---|---|---|
| | /let-ku-jaw/ | lekujaw | 'they won't go' |
| | /ujuk-ja/ | ujuja | 'if you see' |
| | /-kob-kob-en/ | kokoben | 'yearn, long for' |
| | /-tey-tey-or/ | teteyor | 'disentangle' |
| | /jaw-bu-ŋar/ | jabuŋar | 'voyager' |
| | /na-laɲ-laɲ/ | nalalaɲ | 'he returned' |
| | /na-yoken-yoken/ | nayokeyoken | 'he tires' |
| | /na-waɲ-aam-waɲ/ | nwaɲaawaɲ | 'he cultivated for me' |

(i)   What observation can you make about Diola Fogny syllable structure on the basis of the data in (a)?

Simplification does not occur in the following examples, where the first consonant of the cluster is nasal:

b.   /ni-gam-gam/      nigaŋgam      'I judge'
     /ku-boɲ-boɲ/      kubomboɲ      'they sent'
     /na-tiiŋ-tiiŋ/    natiintiiŋ    'he cut through'
     /pan-ji-maɲ/      paɲjimaɲ      'you (pl.) will know'
     /ni-ceɲ-ceɲ/      niceɲceɲ      'I asked'
     /ni-ŋan-ŋan/      niŋaŋŋan      'I cried'

(ii)  Explain the change that occurs in the place of articulation of the nasal.

(iii) Revise your earlier statement about the nature of the possible syllable in Diola Fogny on the basis of the data in (b).

Now consider the forms in (c):

c.   /e-rent-rent/     ererent       'it is light'
     /na-maɲj-maɲj/    namamaɲj      'he knows'

(iv)  How do the data in (c) affect your hypothesis about the Diola Fogny syllable?

EXERCISE **Turkish**
3:9

Consider the following sets of data from Turkish. Each of the sets (a) to (d) exhibit a different phenomenon, although there is a common thread running through the exercise (the data show evidence of the Turkish vowel harmony discussed in chapter 6 of *A Course in Phonology*, but this is irrelevant to the exercise, as is the voicing assimilation in the ablative case):

a.   | *Accusative* | *Nominative* | *Ablative* | |
     |---|---|---|---|
     | hiss+i | his | his+ten | 'feeling' |
     | hakk+ɯ | hak | hak+tan | 'right' |
     | zamm+ɯ | zam | zam+dan | 'price increase' |

(i)   What are the underlying forms of the stems in (a)?

(ii)  Account for the alternating forms.

b.  | Accusative | Nominative | Ablative |
    |---|---|---|
    | devr+i | devir | devir+den | 'transfer' |
    | kojn+u | kojun | kojun+dan | 'bosom' |
    | karn+ɯ | karɯn | karɯn+dan | 'abdomen' |

(iii)   What are the underlying forms of the stems in (b)?

(iv)   Explain why the alternating forms occur.

c.  | Accusative | Nominative | Ablative |
    |---|---|---|
    | zamaːn+ɯ | zaman | zaman+dan | 'time' |
    | iːkaːz+ɯ | iːkaz | iːkaz+dan | 'warning' |
    | ispaːt+ɯ | ispat | ispat+tan | 'proof' |

(v)   Explain the alternations in (c).

d.  | Accusative | Nominative | Ablative |
    |---|---|---|
    | haraːb+ɯ | harap | harap+tan | 'ruined' |
    | ahmed+i | ahmet | ahmet+ten | Ahmed |
    | reng+i | renk | renk+ten | 'colour' |

(vi)   Explain the alternations in (d).

(vii)   What is the common thread running through all the phenomena in data sets (a) to (d)?

EXERCISE **Berber Syllabification**
3:10

In the Imdlawn Tashlhiyt dialect of Berber, spoken in Morocco, any sound may form a syllable nucleus. The sound system of the language is tabulated in (a).

a.   [+consonantal]

| | t | | k | kʷ | q | qʷ | | |
|---|---|---|---|---|---|---|---|---|
| b | d | | g | gʷ | | | | |
| f | s | ʃ | | | χ | χʷ | ħ | |
| | z | ʒ | | | ʁ | ʁʷ | ʕ | ɦ |
| m | n | | | | | | | |
| | l,r | | | | | | | |

[−consonantal]

| | i | u | | a |
|---|---|---|---|---|

(i)    Assuming voiced consonants to be more sonorous than voiceless ones and fricatives to be more sonorous than stops, work out the relative sonority values of all the Berber sounds listed.

(ii)   Following the principles listed below in order of priority, syllabify the forms in (b), where morphemes are separated by hyphens:

b.    /d u-rgaz/      'with the man'             /i-dda u-rgaz/  'the man has come'
      /ra-t-lul-t/    'you will be born'         /kiut/          type of cactus
      /i-iui/         'he brought'               /t-χzn-t/       'you (sg.) stored (pf.)'
      /rks-χ/         'I hid'                     /bain-n/        'they (m.) appear'
      /i-sufu-iit/    'let him illuminate'       /ldi-iii/       'pull me!'
      /ugm-n/         'they (m.) drew (water)'

Principles:

1    The only onsetless syllables allowed are those in absolute initial position; all other syllables must have onsets, in accordance with the Principle of Minimal Onset Satisfaction.

2    Syllable nuclei are formed first from the relatively more sonorous segments in the string, in successive steps.

3    Leftover segments are gathered into codas.

# IV

# Stress

The next level of prosodic structure up from the syllable is made up of metrical feet. Metrical feet define the rhythmic patterns of languages as a function of metrical structure, determined through the assignment of particular settings to the parameters of a universal metrical set. Metrical rhythm is usually manifested through "stress", structured in layers: foot level, word level, phrase level, and perhaps more. The assignment of word stress is subject to principles similar to those that govern the structure of feet. Stress can be restricted on morphosyntactic grounds, as when nouns and verbs, or compounds and phrases, are stressed differently (in English, for instance). Stress (and thus rhythmic structure) is commonly represented by means of a metrical grid, with rows and columns of asterisks: the higher the column, the stronger the stress. Metrical constituents (feet, etc.) are delimited in the grid by means of parentheses, and their head marked by an asterisk in the line immediately above. This formalism allows a very simple and intuitively satisfactory account of stress movement under conditions of clash. Metrical count can be interfered with by "extrametricality", excluding a peripheral element, or by "accent", resulting in stress on an element which would not be stressed otherwise. The effects of syllable weight on metrical configuration receive an alternative formalization in mora theory, with all and only the elements that contribute to syllable weight integrated in the baseline of the metrical grid, which thus replaces the skeleton. Different approaches to metrical structure make use of different additional devices to correct undesirable outputs, among them degenerate foot deletion and line conflation. Not all stress systems are metrical (that is, driven by counting): some build unbounded feet on heavy syllables, and some on purely idiosyncratic syllables marked in the lexicon. In metrical systems, the most common type of foot is binary, but some systems with ternary feet have also been claimed to exist.

# English Rhythm

In chapter 11 we showed the application of the English Rhythm Rule. Consider the following phrases. In some of the cases stress retraction occurs under the influence of the Rhythm Rule and in others it does not. Draw the relevant metrical grids for each of the phrases, showing and explaining why retraction occurs where it does and suggesting the reason for its failure to occur in the other cases.

Diane Price
Elaine Price
Leith High Street
London Road Flyover
kangaroo reservation
kangaroo court
Japanese lantern
Chinese restaurant
Chinese restaurant owner
Grand Central Station
South African President
South African presidential election
malign portent

# Russian Vowel Distribution

Consider the following vowel alternations in Russian (the hook "ˌ" underscripted to some of the consonants indicates a palatalized consonant):

| ṃestə | 'place' | ṃısta | 'places' |
|---|---|---|---|
| feṣt | 'six' | ʃısti | 'six' (gen. dat. prep.) |
| ṇos | 'was taking' (masc.) | ṇısla | 'was taking' (fem.) |
| joʃ | 'hedgehog' | jıʒa | 'hedgehog' (gen. sing.) |
| ʃopət | 'whisper' | ʃıptat | 'to whisper' |

| | | | | |
|---|---|---|---|---|
| ʒonɪ | 'wives' | ʒɪna | 'wife' |
| ʈæɳɪt | 'pulls' | ʈɪnu | 'I pull' |
| tʃas | 'hour' | dva tʃɪsa | 'two o'clock' |
| jadrə | 'nuclei' | jɪdro | 'nucleus' |

(i)   State which vowel alternations occur in these data.

(ii)  Propose a reason for these alternations.

(iii) On the basis of your findings, assign stress to each of the forms provided.


# EXERCISE 4:3   Pintupi

Pintupi is a Pama-Nyungan language from Australia. Consider the following data, where an acute accent indicates primary stress and a grave accent secondary stress:

| | |
|---|---|
| páɳa | 'earth' |
| tʲúʈaya | 'many' |
| máɭawàna | 'through from behind' |
| púɭiŋkàlatʲu | 'we (sat) on the hill' |
| tʲámulùmpatʲùŋku | 'our relation' |
| tʲíɭiriŋulàmpatʲu | 'the fire for our benefit flared up' |
| kúranʲùluìmpatʲùɻa | 'the first one (who is) our relation' |
| yúmaɻiŋkamàratʲùɻaka | 'because of mother-in-law' |

Work out which settings for the parameters FOOT HEAD LOCATION, CON-STRUCTION DIRECTION, EXTRAMETRICALITY and END STRESS yield the correct stress for Pintupi.


# EXERCISE 4:4   Lenakel Stress

In Lenakel (see exercise 3:2 above), apart from those words which have lexically assigned final syllable stress, main stress is penultimate (´ = main stress):

a.   [tɨnágɔl]          'you (sg.) will do it'
     [tɨrébɔl]          'he will then do it'
     [nínɔl]            'you (sg.) have done it'
     [rínɔl]            'he has done it'
     [éheŋ]             'to blow the nose'
     [rɨmáwŋɨn]         'he ate'
     [nápuk]            'lungs'
     [tɨkómkom]     '   'branches'

Subsidiary stress positions are calculated differently depending on the grammatical
category of the form in question (` = subsidiary stress):

b.   *Nouns*
     [tupʷàlukáluk]        'lungs'
     [lètupʷàlukáluk]      'in the lungs'
     [nèlujáɲjaŋ]          'twig'
     [kajèlawélaw]         'kind of dance'

c.   *Verbs*
     [rɨmolkéjkej]                'you (pl.) liked it'
     [nɨmarolkéjkej]              'you (pl.) were liking it'
     [tɨnakàrolkéjkej]            'you (pl.) will be liking it'
     [nàdjagàmetwàtamnímʷan]      'why am I about to be shaking?'

Work out the stress algorithm(s) responsible for:

(i)    main stress;

(ii)   subsidiary stresses in nouns and in verbs.

# EXERCISE 4:5   The English Stress Algorithm

The place names listed below have been plucked from an atlas of Africa. How
would an English speaker apply stress to these words? In some of the cases there
is more than one possible stress pattern: where would you place the main stress and
the subsidiary stress(es) on these words? Explain, through the application of the English stress algorithm, how you arrived at your own stress pattern. See if you can also
explain what other patterns are possible and how the provisions of the algorithm
can predict this variation.

Ambatofinandrahana
Madukani
Dimbelenge
Semalambo
Kinsenia
Nyamtukusa
Bongandanga
Garissa
Mogincual
Mahalapye
Naboamspruit
Ambodifototra
Ferkessedougou

## EXERCISE Creek
## 4:6

Creek is a Muskogean language of Oklahoma and Florida. We list examples of placement of tonal accent (main stress) in what are described by Hayes (1995) as "simplex words". (NB: Building feet on moras will help with the answers.)

a.     ifá             'dog'
       tsokó          'house'
       amífa          'my dog'
       ifótsi           'puppy'
       amifotsí       'my puppy'
       apataká        'pancake'
       amapatáka     'my pancake'
       anokitsíta       'to love'
       amanokitsitá    'to love mine'
       itiwanajipíta    'to tie each other'

(i)    Work out the stress algorithm for the forms in (a) taking account of such factors as foot shape, direction of foot construction, and line conflation.

b.     fóː           'bee'
       niháː        'lard'
       hoktíː       'woman'
       hitotíː      'snow'

tiːniːtkíː    'thunder'

(ii)     Can the forms in (b) be accounted for by the same algorithm as those in (a)?
         Why?

c.       tsáːlo          'trout'
         ítski           'mother'
         potsóswa        'axe'
         kofótska        'mint'
         famíːtsa        'canteloupe'
         alakkójtska     'appreciation'

(iii)    Can your current algorithm also account for the forms in (c)? Why?

d.       aktopá          'bridge'
         taːskitá        'to jump' (sg. subj.)
         waːkotsí        'calf'
         atiloːjitá      'to gather' (pl. obj.)
         iŋkosapitá      'one to implore'
         nafkitikaːjitá  'to hit' (pl. obj.)
         jakaphojíta     'two to walk'
         tokoɬhokíta     'to run' (dual subj.)
         alpatótsi       'baby alligator'

(iv)     Do the data in (d) add anything to our understanding? Explain.

Now sum up your results by answering the following questions:

(v)      Is Creek quantity sensitive?

(vi)     What counts as a heavy syllable in Creek?

(vii)    Does Creek have extrametricality?

(viii)   What is the direction of foot construction?

(ix)     Are feet right- or left-headed?

(x)      How does End Stress apply?

(xi)     Does conflation apply?

## EXERCISE Hindi
## 4:7

Consider the following examples of what look like very complicated Hindi stress patterns, outlined in Hayes (1995):

a.   Stress the initial syllable of a disyllabic word:
    [bála]        'force'
    [kálaː]       'art'
    [ʧúːɽaː]     'bangle'
    [kámal]     'lotus'
    [ráːʤan]    (proper name)

b.   Stress a heavy penult:
    [asúːʤʰaː]   'invisible'

c.   Otherwise, stress a heavy antepenult:
    [bándʰana]   'binding'
    [insáːnijat]   'humanness'

d.   Otherwise the preantepenultimate if the final is light:
    [ánumati]   'permission'

e.   Or the antepenult if the final is heavy; or in trisyllables:
    [titálijaː]   'butterfly'
    [áditi]     (proper name)
    [ámitaː]    (proper name)

(i)    Is Hindi quantity-sensitive?

(ii)   Are feet right-headed or left-headed?

(iii)  What is the direction of foot construction?

(iv)  Are degenerate feet stressed?

(v)   Does extrametricality apply? To what constituent? Left or right?

(vi)  Does End Stress apply?

When you have answered questions (i) to (vi), apply the algorithm to the data in (a) to (e).

# EXERCISE 4:8 A Japanese Language Game

The language game *Shiritori* is played by children throughout Japan. The players take turns thinking of a word that begins with the last sound unit of the word given by the previous player. "N" is a "moraic nasal" that may render a syllable heavy and takes its place features by assimilation with the following consonant. When it occurs prepausally it may surface as a uvular nasal [N]. The game proceeds as in (a) and (b) below:

a.  tubame   'swallow'  →  medaka  'killifish'   →  kao    'face'  →
    oNgaku   'music'    →  kusari   'medicine'   →  riNgo  apple  →
    gohaN    'meal' (end of game)

b.  budoo 'grapes'  →  origami 'folding-paper'  →  miNku 'mink'  →
    kuuki 'air'  →  kiriN  'giraffe' (end of game)

(i)   What is the "last sound unit of a word" in prosodic terms?

(ii)  Why should the words *gohaN* and *kiriN* finish the game?

The examples in (c) are never observed as legitimate in *Shiritori*:

c.  budoo 'grape'  →  *doobutu 'animal'
    soNgokuu  (character in a Chinese fairy tale)  →  *kuuki 'air'

(iii) Do the data in (c) confirm your hypothesis about the "sound units"?

(iv)  In chapter 13 of *A Course in Phonology* we offer two alternative models for syllable–mora relationship: which of these do the Japanese data favour?

# EXERCISE 4:9 Stress in Malayalam

Malayalam is a Dravidian language spoken in Kerala, in southern India. According to Mohanan (1986), the evidence for stress in the language is that unstressed vowels are centralized and reduced in duration (possibly even deleting in casual speech). Primary and secondary stresses (where appropriate) are marked in the data below (long segments are indicated by geminates):

| | | | |
|---|---|---|---|
| kářaṭi | 'bear' | káařaṇam | 'reason' |
| kařáarǝ | 'agreement' | páṭṭaṇam | 'town' |
| páaṭṭa | 'bucket' | paṭṭáaḷam | 'army' |
| mářaṇam | 'death' | páařàayaṇam | 'reading' |
| aŋgáařasàaṭmìikařaṇam | | 'carbon assimilation' | |

(i)    Is Malayalam quantity sensitive?

(ii)   Are Malayalam feet bounded or unbounded?

(iii)  Are feet right- or left-headed?

(iv)   Are degenerate feet permitted?

(v)    On the basis of the answers to (i) to (iv), construct a stress algorithm for Malayalam and show how it assigns the correct stress patterns in the data given.


# EXERCISE 4:10    Tübatulabal

Prince (1983) gives the following information about Tübatulabal, a Uto-Aztecan language of Southern California.

The stress patterns are as follows:

a.    Final syllables are always stressed.

b.    Long vowels are always stressed.

c.    Some stresses are fixed in certain morphemes.

d.    In a stretch of short-vowelled syllables not stressed by (a) or (c) above, stress alternates right to left.

According to Hayes (1995):

e.    Main stress is on the final syllable.

| | |
|---|---|
| witàŋhatál | 'the Tejon Indians' |
| wìtaŋhàtalà:batsú | 'away from the Tejon Indians' |
| jù:dù:jù:dát | 'the fruit is mashing' |

| tìkapìganàjín | 'the one who was eating'; /piganá/ = recent past agentive |
| hanìːlá | 'the house' (obj.) |
| waʃàːgàhajá | 'it might flame up' |
| ànaɲìːnìnimút | 'he is crying wherever he goes' (distr.) |

(i)    Translate the information above into the provisions of a stress algorithm.

(ii)   Work through the words in (a) applying the provisions as you have outlined them.

(iii)  What is the definition of the heavy syllable in Tübatulabal?

(iv)   Work out the stress patterns of the words below:

| eleːgɨt | 'he is looking out' |
| hatdaːwahabi | 'you may cross it' |
| anaŋaːlilɔːgɔpɨganan | 'he is the one who was going along pretending to cry' |

# V

# Tone

No language is normally delivered in a flat pitch: on the contrary, speech is usually "sung". Such singing involves the alternation of different pitch levels, readily formalizable (simplifying a bit) as the association of the elements H(igh), L(ow) and M(id) to certain segments, usually syllable nuclei. These elements are technically known as "tones". There are several ways in which tones can be structured in language. First, tonal patterns can be used to differentiate lexical items with an identical segmental makeup. Tonal languages of this kind abound, and are spread over at least four of the globe's five continents, even at present. Second, tonal patterns can be used to express functional or attitudinal meaning. Such use of tonal patterns is commonly referred to as "intonation", and typically occurs in the languages of Europe, although naturally not only there. Finally, some other languages have one, or at most a small number, of what can be construed as meaningless intonational patterns, which are systematically associated to each word domain, or to the words of a certain category. These languages are known as "pitch accent" languages. The autosegmental mode of representation provides a particularly apposite tool for the analysis of tonal phenomena. Indeed, autosegmental phonology was developed in the context of tone and intonation, African tone systems in particular. The principles of autosegmental association, particularly in their original formulation, thus reflect the structure of these African languages. However, the subsequent refinement of these principles extends them to a wider autosegmental context (cf. the No-Crossing of Lines constraint, for instance). As in other aspects of phonology, the initial association of tones to segments can be subject to subsequent modification by rule. There is solid evidence for tones which are real but are not associated to any particular segment (cf. downstep), a situation that strongly endorses the autosegmental model.

# Yala Ikom Reduplication

Consider the following data from Yala Ikom, a Kwa language of Nigeria with three surface tones (H = ´; L = `; M = ¯):

a.  à nyì       'you buried'            b.   ò + nyī + nyì          'burying'
    à bī        'you carried'                ò + bī + bī            'carrying'
    à hàrà      'you accompanied'            ɔ̀ + hārā + hàrà        'accompanying'

The forms in (b) suggest that gerunds are formed via stem reduplication segmentally, and M insertion tonally. Now consider the stem !gbèhē 'chop' and its gerund ɔ̀gbèhēgbèhē 'chopping'.

(i)   Provide the autosegmental representation of the stem for 'chop'.

(ii)  Can the gerund for 'chopping' be derived in the same manner as the other gerunds?

(iii) What does this derivation tell us about the status of M in Yala Ikom?

# Mixtecan

Mixtecan is an Oto-Manguean language spoken in the Mexican state of Oaxaca. In the San Miguel El Grande variety there are three surface tones (H, M, L), which occur unrestrictedly in disyllables, except for the pattern LL, which doesn't show up:

a.  sáná       'turkey'            HH
    ɲíʔī       'steam bath'        HM
    báʔù       'coyote'            HL
    kūtʃí       'pig'              MH
    bēʔē       'house'             MM

|        |          |    |
|--------|----------|----|
| kòò    | 'snake'  | ML |
| sùʧí   | 'child'  | LH |
| mìnī   | 'puddle' | LM |

The postposition of a word like *sùʧí* 'child' to *kēē* 'go away' gives the expected outcome:

b.   kēē sùʧí   'the child will go away'

However, when *sùʧí* is postposed to the homophonous *kēē* 'eat', its first tone undergoes change:

c.   kēē súʧí   'the child will eat'

The phenomenon is also triggered by words of grammatical categories other than verbs, including the noun *sùʧí* itself:

| d.  | bīnā | 'today' | nì-hīnì-ná ɔ̄ɔ̄n sùʧí bínā | 'I saw a child today' |
|-----|------|---------|---------------------------|------------------------|
|     | máá  | 'that'  | máá súʧí                  | 'that child'           |
| cf. | tàká | 'all'   | tàká sùʧí                 | 'all the children'     |

Lexical tone patterns other than LH can also be subject to change:

| e. | kòò | 'snake' | kēē kóò       | 'the snake will eat'     |
|----|-----|---------|---------------|--------------------------|
|    |     |         | cf. kēē kòò   | 'the snake will go away' |

However, words with lexical HH, HM and HL remain unchanged:

| f. | sáná | 'turkey' | kēē sáná  | 'the turkey will go away' |
|----|------|----------|-----------|----------------------------|
|    |      |          | kēē sáná  | 'the turkey will eat'      |
|    | báʔù | 'coyote' | kēē báʔù  | 'the coyote will go away'  |
|    |      |          | kēē báʔù  | 'the coyote will eat'      |

We ask you to devise an analysis that accounts for the state of affairs described through exclusively phonological means. (Hint: lexical tones may be invisible in the surface.)

# EXERCISE 5:3   Venda Tones

The tonal shape of nominals in the South African Bantu language Venda varies according to the position of the nominals in a phrase. The language has three tones, high (acute accent ´ ), low (grave accent ` ) and falling (circumflex accent ^). Consider the following pairs:

| a. | *In isolation and after a surface low tone* | b. | *After a surface high tone (e.g. ndìvhóná ___ 'I see ___')* | |
|---|---|---|---|---|
| | mù-tùkà | | mú-tûkà | 'youth' |
| | mù-ràthú | | mú-râthú | 'brother' |
| | mù-sélwà | | mú-sêlwà | 'bride' |
| | mù-sádzí | | mú-sâdzì | 'woman' |

The correct tonal contour can be obtained on the forms above by the ordered application of three rules:

L-deletion:      L → Ø / H [ ___

Meussen's Law:  H → L / H _____

H-spread:        V      V
                 |........·
                 H

(i)    Propose underlying representations for (b).

(ii)   Give the derivations of each of the post-high forms listed above.

(iii)  Why doesn't Meussen's Law apply in *mù-sádzí*? (Hint: Meussen's Law requires a *sequence* of Hs.)

## EXERCISE 5:4 Croatian Dialects

Neo-Stokavian Croatian dialects of Serbo-Croatian contain pitch patterns such as the following (´ = H; ` = L):

a.  nébò        'sky'
    súùʃà       'dry season'
    kráàj       'country'
    súùntʃàtì   'to sunbathe'
    vjérùjèèm   'I can believe'
    máàrvà      'cattle'
    kráàʎ       'king'

(i)   Assuming that the forms in (a) carry H in the lexicon, provide a formal account of their pitch patterns.

b.  dànás       'today'
    nògá        'foot'
    glìistá     'worm'
    mlàatítì    'to beat'
    djèvòòjká   'girl'
    nògèè       'leg' (gen.)
    pèèták      'Friday'

(ii)  Assuming that the forms in (b) have an underlying LH melody, how can the surface forms shown be accounted for?

(iii) Sum up the tonal similarities and differences between the classes in (a) and (b).

## EXERCISE 5:5 Osaka Japanese

The pitch patterns of Osaka Japanese differ from those of Tokyo Japanese, which we examine in chapter 14 of *A Course in Phonology*. Consider the following forms of Osaka Japanese (*-ga* is an enclitic particle marking the nominative; ´ = H; ` = L; ^ = HL):

a.   àmê        'rain'       àmé-gà
     kàbútò     'helmet'     kàbútò-gà
     màttî      'match'      màttí-gà
     bìtámìn    'vitamin'    bìtámìn-gà
     nòkògírì   'saw'        nòkògírì-gà

(i)     Can you propose an underlying pitch melody for Osaka Japanese on the
        basis of these data?

(ii)    Which syllable would be accented in each of these words?

(iii)   How would the mapping between tones and vowels proceed?

Now consider the following forms:

b.   èé         'picture'    è-gá
     sòrá       'sky'        sòrà-gá
     sùzùmé     'sparrow'    sùzùmè-gá
     tùkèmònó   'pickles'    tùkèmònò-gá

(iv)    Can you see the difference(s) between these forms and their predecessors?

(v)     Do these forms force the postulation of a different pitch melody or can they
        be accounted for with a simple contextual operation on the pitch melody
        needed for the previous set?

In (c) we provide a final data set:

c.   éé         'handle'     é-gá
     náà        'name'       ná-gà
     táké       'bamboo'     táké-gá
     yámà       'mountain'   yámà-gà
     ótókò      'man'        ótókò-gà
     níwátórí   'chicken'    níwátórí-gá

(vi)    Does this set warrant an additional underlying pitch melody?

(vii)   What will the accented vowel be (if any) in each of the forms in (c)?

(viii)  Provide the corresponding derivations.

# EXERCISE 5:6 Gernika Basque Pitch Accent

The variety of Basque spoken in the town of Gernika and the surrounding area presents an example of pitch accent which exhibits, at least, a superficial similarity to the Japanese we discuss in chapter 14 of *A Course in Phonology*. Consider the examples in (a) (taken from the source and given mainly in standard Basque orthography; ´ = H; ` = L):

a.

| absolutive singular /-a/ | plural /-àk/ | indefinite /-Ø/ | |
|---|---|---|---|
| gìxóná | gìxónàk | gìxón | 'man' |
| làgúné | làgúnèk | làgún | 'friend' |
| gùntzúrrúné | gùntzúrrúnèk | gùntzúrrún | 'kidney' |
| txìstúláįʒé | txìstúláįèk | txìstúláį | 'flautist' |
| nèskíé | néskàk | nèská | 'girl' |
| ètzíé | ètzíèk | ètzé | 'house' |
| mèndíʒé | mèndíʒèk | mèndí | 'mountain' |
| lùrré | lúrrèk | lúr | 'land, ground' |
| àrrá | árràk | ár | 'worm' |

(i)   Describe the three tonal patterns in (a).

(ii)  Formalize the procedures which will derive the correct pitch accent patterns for the noun forms in (a). (Hint: the stem lexical pitch melody is simply H.)

Now consider the dative forms in (b):

b.

| dative singular /-ari/ | plural /-àri/ | indefinite /-ri/ |
|---|---|---|
| gìxónárí | gìxónàrì | gìxónérí |
| làgúnérí | làgúnèrì | làgúnérí |
| gùntzúrrúnérí | gùntzúrrúnèrì | gùntzúrrúnérí |

(iii) Explain the difference between the singular and plural dative forms. Show how the association procedure you have set up derives these forms.

# EXERCISE 5:7 Yoruba

Yoruba, a Kwa language mainly spoken in Nigeria and Benin, has three contrastive surface tones H, M, L: cf. *kɔ́* 'build', *kɔ̄* 'sing', *kɔ̀* 'refuse'. Contour tones are derived, as illustrated in the abstract paradigms in (a) and (b), where non-existent forms are starred:

a. CV́ CV́
   CV́ CV̂
   *CV́ CV̀

b. CV̀ CV̀
   CV̀ CV̌
   *CV̀ CV́

(i) On the basis of these paradigms, provide a formal account of the contour tones of Yoruba.

In connected speech, one of two abutting vowels gets deleted:

c. ʃē īʃé  →  ʃīʃé      'do work (= work)'
   mū ēmū  →  mēmū      'drink palm-wine'
   pā ējò  →  pējò      'kill a snake'

Of interest to us here is the fate of the tone of the deleted vowel. Consider the following set of data:

d. kɔ́ èkɔ̄  →  kêkɔ̄      'learn a lesson'
   rí ɔ̀bē  →  rɔ̂bē      'see a knife'
   rí àpò  →  râpò      'see a bag'

(ii) Provide the derivation of the connected speech forms in this set and in (c).

In Standard Yoruba the forms in (d) simplify further, as follows:

e. kékɔ̄
   rɔ́!bē
   rápò

(iii) Propose a tone rule to account for the Standard Yoruba forms in (e).

Now consider two additional sets of data:

f. rí īgbá  →  rígbá      'see a calabash'
   rí āʃɔ̄  →  ráʃɔ̄      'see cloth'
   rí ɔ̀bè  →  rɔ́bê      'see soup'

g. ʃē ɔ̌rɛ̌  →  ʃɔ̌rɛ̌      'be friends'
   pā ɔ̄bɔ́  →  pɔ̀bɔ́     'kill a monkey'
   ʃē ɔ́fɔ́  →  ʃɔ́fɔ́     'mourn'

(iv)  Propose now an overall account of Yoruba tonology as represented in the data provided. Pay particular attention to two issues: (1) the specific status of M; (2) whether or not Yoruba tones are already associated underlyingly.

## EXERCISE 5:8  Nzema

In Nzema, a Volta-Comoe language spoken in Ghana and the Ivory Coast, nouns in isolation exhibit one of two surface tonal patterns (an asterisk after a tone indicates that the tone matches the number of available vowels):

a.  L*H                                    b.  L*
     èzèká?      'comb'                         èsùpà?      'bed'
    èbònú?      'forest'                        àgòlè?      'dance'
    èwɔlèɣá     'star'                          kèlènè      'frog'
    ŋwàá        'tale'                          sù.à        'house'
    àdèlé?      'spoon'                         bànè?       'wall'
    bɔlé        'luggage'                       àlùgbà      'beans'
    èlù.é       'yam'                           bàkà?       'tree'
    kùlùkwé?    'calabash'                      àzùlè       'river'

(i)   Provide an autosegmental representation for these patterns.

The set in (a) splits into (c) and (d) before the postposed demonstrative yé 'this':

c.  L*H
    èzèká yé          'this comb'

d.  L*HĹ
    kùlùkwê yé        'this calabash'

(ii)  State in what way the set in (a) has split into (c) and (d).

Now consider the general tonal behaviour of the word /kɔ̄/ 'one', also postposed to the noun:

e.    èzèká        'comb'        èzèká kɔ́        'one comb'
      kúsù         'cat'         kúsù kɔ̂        'one cat'

f.    kùlùkwéʔ     'calabash'    kùlùkwé kɔ̂     'one calabash'
      èsùpàʔ       'bed'         èsùpà kɔ́       'one bed'

(iii)   How does *kɔ* acquire its tone in (e)?

(iv)    Does this have a bearing on the lexical tonal representation of the words for 'calabash' and 'bed' in (f)?

(v)     Provide a formal account of all the processes reported.

# EXERCISE 5:9    Karanga Shona

Shona is a Bantu language spoken in Zimbabwe. The following facts specifically refer to the Karanga dialect.

The diminutive suffix is *-àná*, with a low tone on the first vowel and a high tone on the second vowel. Upon suffixation, the first *a* of this suffix combines with the final stem vowel to make up one syllable (the details of the vowel combination are irrelevant to our concerns here). On the basis of this information:

(i)     Propose lexical tone melodies for the base forms in the set in (a), italicized to indicate that their representations are incomplete, with the tones still missing.

(ii)    Propose a rule to explain how the surface tone pattern is derived (hint: Shona has neither surface contour tones nor downstep):

a.    *mwana* + àná   →   mwànáná        'little child'
      *dhongi* + àná  →   dhòngwáná      'little donkey'
      *dengu* + àná   →   dèngwáná       'little basket'

(iii)   In what way does the set of data in (b) contradict the findings so far (you can ignore the segmental alternations for the purposes of this exercise)?:

b.    hárí      'pot'   →   hádyàná
      mbúdzí    'goat'  →   mbúdzàná
      mùrúmé    'man'   →   mùrúnyàná ('brother-in-law')

(iv)   Provide autosegmental representations for the forms in (b) and compare them with the ones for (a).

(v)    Propose a further rule to explain why the low tone persists on the first vowel of -*àná* in (b).

Assuming that the verbal habitual prefix *no-* is characterized in the lexicon by a falling tone HL, consider the data in (c):

c.     ndì-nó-bìkà      'I cook'
       tì-nó-bìkà       'we cook'
       ndì-nó-tórá      'I take'
       tì-nó-tórá       'we take'

(vi)   Can the first of your two rules explain why the habitual prefix simplifies as H?

Consider now a final set:

d.     á-nò-bìkà        'he cooks'
       vá-nò-bìkà       'they cook'
       á-nò-tórá        'he takes'

(vii)  Are the data in (d) automatically accounted for by the machinery you have built, in conjunction with the universal principles? (Hint: the vowel preceding *nò* in (d) carries a high tone.)


EXERCISE **Cantonese**
5:10

Cantonese is a Yue language spoken in the province of Guangdong and in Hong Kong, in the People's Republic of China. Of the three Cantonese basic tones H, M and L, H or L can appear in *binary* combination with M (Cantonese thus does not allow contour tones or tones spanning the full pitch range). We partially illustrate the situation in (a) with proper nouns:

a.

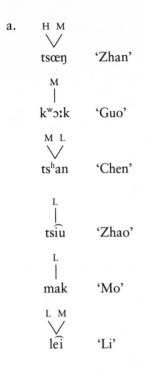

|  |  |
|---|---|
| H M<br>∨<br>tsœŋ | 'Zhan' |
| M<br>\|<br>kʷɔːk | 'Guo' |
| M L<br>∨<br>tsʰan | 'Chen' |
| L<br>\|<br>tsi͡u | 'Zhao' |
| L<br>\|<br>mak | 'Mo' |
| L M<br>∨<br>le͡i | 'Li' |

The language has the vocative prefixes *a* and *lo͡u*. In (b) we illustrate the surface effect of prefixing these elements to some of the nouns in (a), in conjunction with a purely tonal familiar vocative suffix H:

b.

|  |  |  |
|---|---|---|
| M  H<br>\|  \|<br>a tsœŋ | 'old Zhan!' | ('old' = sign of familiarity) |
| L M  M H<br>∨    ∨<br>lo͡u kʷɔːk | 'old Guo!' | |
| M  M H<br>\|  ∨<br>a tsʰan | 'old Chen!' | |

(i)    What is the underlying tonal representation of the forms in (b)?

(ii)   Account for the tone changes in (b) in a unified manner, as simple and natural as possible. (Hint: bear in mind the restrictions on tone combinations mentioned at the outset.)

In (c) we give the vocative forms of the remainder of the nouns in (a):

c.    M M H

a tsiu       'old Zhao!'

L M M H

lou mak     'old Mo!'

L M M H

lou lei      'old Li!'

(iii)  Are these tonal patterns predicted by the account you gave for (b)?

(iv)  If not, what do you have to add to your analysis to account for them?

# VI

# The Interaction between Morphology and Phonology

Phonological rules often affect words, or larger domains, in stages determined by their structure: they first apply in the smallest, or innermost, constituent, and then in successively larger ones. This mode of application of rules is commonly known as "the cycle", and the rules in question are said to be "cyclic" and to apply "cyclically". The domain of each cycle has long been thought to be defined by the grammatical structure of the form, say, by the morphemes that make up a word (stem, suffixes, prefixes). The theory of the cycle has found particularly successful application in suprasegmental areas: for instance, in tonal phonology or in metrical phonology. In segmental phonology the application of the cycle has often been indirect, via the blocking effect of the Principle of Strict Cyclicity. In many, perhaps all, languages, the outer structural layers of words, as defined by certain affixes, are not subject to cyclic rules. This means that, for the purposes of the phonology, words (and perhaps other grammatical domains) need to be layered in a manner that goes beyond the constituents made available by the grammar. The theory that concerns itself with such additional levels, or "strata", is known as Lexical Phonology. According to Lexical Phonology, each affix is idiosyncratically assigned to a certain stratum, in which certain phonological rules apply, also idiosyncratically or as a result of their interaction with universal principles of rule application. One important consequence of Lexical Phonology, at least in its classical formulation, is that word-construction processes can be sensitive to the output of a phonological rule in a previous stratum. Domains larger than the word are formalized as additional strata ("postlexical strata"), with properties distinct from the lexical strata.

**German**

# 6:1

In German [ç] and [x] are in complementary distribution, as we show in (a) and (b):

a.  
| siech | [ziːç] | 'sickly' |
|---|---|---|
| ich | [ɪç] | 'I' |
| Pech | [pɛç] | 'bad luck' |
| euch | [ɔʏç] | 'you' (fam. pl. acc./dat.) |
| reich | [raɪç] | 'rich' |
| Büchlein | [byːçlaɪn] | 'booklet' |
| Wöchnerin | [vœçnərɪn] | 'maternity case' |
| höchlich | [høçlɪç] | 'highly' |

b.  
| Buch | [buːx] | 'book' |
|---|---|---|
| Spruch | [ʃprʊx] | 'saying' |
| Koch | [kɔx] | 'cook' |
| hoch | [hoːx] | 'high' |
| Hauch | [haʊx] | 'breath' |
| nach | [naːx] | 'after' |
| Bach | [bax] | 'brook' |

(i)   What determines which of the two fricatives will occur?

(ii)   Is it possible to determine which of the two alternants is lexical?

Now consider the forms in (c) and (d):

c.  
| solch | [zɔlç] | 'such a' |
|---|---|---|
| manch | [manç] | 'many a' |
| durch | [dʊrç] | 'through' |
| Dolche | [dɔlç] | 'daggers' |
| mancher | [mançər] | 'many a' (masc.) |
| schnarchen | [ʃnarçən] | 'to snore' |

d.  
| Chemie | [çemiː] | 'chemistry' |
|---|---|---|
| Chirurg | [çirʊrk] | 'surgeon' |
| Cholesterin | [çɔlɛsteriːn] | 'cholesterol' |
| Charisma | [çarɪsma] | 'charisma' |

(iii)   How do the examples in (c) and (d) affect your hypothesis?

(iv)   Propose a rule to encapsulate the alternation.

In the light of what you have proposed so far, consider the minimal pairs in (e):

e.   Kuchen      [kuːxən]      'cake'
     tauchen     [taʊxən]      'to dive'        (tauch+en)
     pfauchen    [p͡faʊxən]     'to hiss'        (pfauch+en)
     Kuhchen     [kuːçən]      'little cow'     (Kuh+chen)
     Tauchen     [taʊçən]      'little rope'    (Tau+chen)
     Pfauchen    [p͡faʊçən]     'little peacock' (Pfau+chen)

(v)    Do these forms indicate that our original claim about [ç] and [x] being in complementary distribution was incorrect?

(vi)   What is the crucial difference in the position of the relevant sound between these pairs?

(vii)  Revise your procedure to take account of the additional information.


# EXERCISE 6:2   Ponapean

The following data from the Austronesian language Ponapean show the results of the concatenation of segments sharing a place or articulation:

a.   *Suffixed forms*
     /weid-da/    →   [weidida]      'proceed upward'
     /lus-saŋ/    →   [lusisaŋ]      'jump from'

b.   *Prefixed forms*
     /ep-pʷoatol/    →   [amʷpʷoatol]   'game'
     /sapʷ-paa/      →   [sampaa]       'world, earth'
     /ak-keelail/    →   [aŋkeelail]    'demonstrate strength'

c.   *Reduplicated forms*
     /pap-pap/    →   [pampap]      'swimming'
     /kik-kik/    →   [kiŋkik]      'kicking'
     /tat-tat/    →   [tantat]      'writhe'
     /sas-sas/    →   [sansas]      'stagger'

| /dil-dil/ | → | [dindil] | 'penetrate' |
| /sel-sel/ | → | [sensel] | 'tied' |
| /sar-sar/ | → | [sansar] | 'fade' |

(i)   How does the process in (a) differ from those in (b) and (c)?

(ii)   Write rules to show the relationship between the lexical and phonetic forms.

Now consider the examples in (d):

d.

| /kiassi/ | → | [kiassi] | 'catcher' |
| /kakko/ | → | [kakko] | 'putting on airs' |
| /nappa/ | → | [nappa] | 'Chinese cabbage' |
| /rerrer/ | → | [rerrer] | 'to be trembling' |

(iii)   What would your rules have predicted the phonetic forms of the words in (c) would be? What does their actual phonetic form tell us about the status of the rules with regard to cyclicity and why?

# EXERCISE 6:3   Polish

There is a very productive rule in Polish which causes coronal consonants to be palatalized when they precede front vowels (/i/ and /e/), both in native vocabulary and loanwords. The result is as we show below:

a.

| s | z | | ç | ʑ |
| t | d | → | tç | dʑ |
| n | | | ɲ | |

Some examples are shown in (b) (data are given in Polish orthography unless otherwise indicated):

b.

| Masc. nom. sg. | | Loc. sg. | Verb |
|---|---|---|---|
| gryma[s] | 'wry face' | gryma[ç+i]e | gryma[ç+i+tç] |
| nawó[z] | 'fertilizer' | nawo[ʑ+i]e | nawo[ʑ+i+tç] |
| kształ[t] | 'shape' | kształ[tç+i]e | ksztal[tç+i+tç] |
| głó[d] | 'hunger' | gło[dʑ+i]e | gło[dʑ+i+tç] |
| ukło[n] | 'bow' | ukło[ɲ+i]e | ukło[ɲ+i+tç] |

|  |  | *Masc. nom. pl.* |
|---|---|---|
| szwe[d] | 'Swede' | szwe[dʑi] |
| lingwi[st] | 'linguist' | lingwi[ɕtɕi] |
| intru[z] | 'intruder' | intru[ʑi] |
| dżentelme[n] | 'gentleman' | dżentelme[ɲi] |

However, coronal palatalization fails to occur in cases like the following:

c.  pro[te]st          'protest'
    ul[ti]mat+um       'ultimatum'
    [de]sant           'landing'
    [di]nosaur         'dinosaur'
    [se]kund           'second'
    mak[si]m+um        'maximum'

(i)  Suggest an explanation for the failure of the forms in (c) to undergo palatalization.

Now, consider the examples in (d):

d.  *Nominative*                    *Locative*
    servi[s]    'service'           servi[ɕ+e]
    te[z]a      'thesis'            te[ʑ+e]

                                    *Diminutive*
    te[st]      'test'             te[ɕtɕ+ik]
    silo[s]     'silo'             s'ilo[ɕ+ik]

(ii)  How do the data in (d) confirm your hypothesis?


# EXERCISE 6:4   Vedic Sanskrit

In chapter 13 of *A Course in Phonology* we present the stress pattern of Vedic Sanskrit and explain that, in this language, some morphemes, stems and suffixes are lexically accented, whilst others are inherently unaccented. We also discovered that foot construction is disallowed. A word only contains one stressed syllable, indicated by an acute accent on the vowel (ś = voiceless alveolopalatal fricative). The basic stress rule of Vedic Sanskrit is as follows:

> Stress the leftmost accented syllable (if there is one), otherwise stress the leftmost syllable.

Examples are shown in (a), where lexically accented vowels are underlined:

a.  áśvan̯am          'horses'
    deván̯am          'gods'
    áśv̯avatin̯am      'having horses'
    padvatiná̱m       'having feet'
    dúhitar          'daughter' (vocative)
    duhitré̱          'daughter' (dat. sg.)
    bhrátar          'brother' (vocative)
    bhrátre̱          'brother' (dat. sg.)
    marút            'wind' (vocative)
    marúte̱           'wind' (dat. sg.)

(i)   Show how stress is correctly located in the forms in (a).

The suffixes of Vedic Sanskrit are divided into two sets, dubbed "dominant" and "recessive". Consider the placement of stress in the suffixed forms below, where the subscript $_D$ denotes a dominant morpheme and the subscript $_R$ a recessive one (as before, accented vowels are underlined):

b.  $ra̱th+in_D+e_R$                  →  rathíne          'charioteer' (dat. sg.)
    $mitr+in_D+e_R$                  →  mitríne          'befriended' (dat. sg.)
    $sar+as_D+vat_R+i_R+vant_R$      →  sárasvativant    'accompanied by Sarasvati'
    $prati+cyav+iyas_D+i_R$          →  práticyaviyasi   'more compressed'
    $kār+a̱y_D+itum_D$               →  kárayitum        'in order to cause to make'
    $ci+kār+a̱y_D+iṣa_D+ti_R$        →  cíkārayiṣati     'wants to cause to make'

(ii)  Show how the stress patterns of the forms in (b) can be derived from the basic stress rule given above, in the context of the stress cycle and of Lexical Phonology, as expounded in chapter 16 of *A Course in Phonology* (NB you will have to make a certain assumption about (a) to get the procedure to work).

# EXERCISE 6:5  Chamorro Stress Assignment

Primary stress in non-complex (un-derived) words in the Western Austronesian language Chamorro is assigned on one of the last three syllables of the word (transcriptions follow Chung 1983, except for "y" = [j], "ä" = [æ], "ñ" = [ɲ]):

a.    *Final: Spanish loanwords*
       lugót          'place'
       syudó          'city'
       peskadót       'fisherman'
       kafé           'coffee'
       muntón         'swarm'
       kimasón        'to burn'

b.    *Antepenultimate: Some native and a large number of loan words*
       mámati         'reef'
       píkaru         'sly'
       dóŋkulu        'big'
       éntaluʔ        'middle'
       kúnanaf        'to crawl'
       éŋŋuluʔ        'to peep'

c.    *Penultimate: All other words*
       pulónnun       'trigger fish'
       aságʷa         'spouse'
       inéksaʔ        'cooked rice'
       paníti         'to strike'
       bilimbínis     'star-apple'
       kítan          'cross-eyed'
       púgʷaʔ         'betel nut'
       lémmaj         'breadfruit'

(i)   Show how these stress patterns can be accounted for, making use of the devices discussed in chapters 12 and 13 of *A Course in Phonology*.

Consider now the following suffixed forms shown with their stems:

d.    nóna           'mother'       nanóhu           'my mother'
       gúmaʔ          'house'        gumóʔmu          'your (sg.) house'
       sóŋan          'to say'       saŋóni           'to say to'
       dóŋkulu        'big'          daŋkulónña       'bigger'
       finalógu       'running'      finalangúña      'his running'
       inéŋŋuluʔ      'peeping'      ineŋŋuluʔníha    'their peeping'
       bapót          'ship'         bapotníha        'their ship'

(ii)  How can the stress shift in the suffixed forms be accounted for?

Prefixes in Chamorro fall into two categories, those which do not change the stress of the stem:

e.  géftaw      'generous'      mangéftaw      'generous' (pl.)
    díkiki?      'small'         mandíkiki?     'small' (pl.)
    kádada?      'short'         na?kádada?     'to shorten'
                                 mana?kádada?   'to be shortened'
    fa?gósi      'to wash'       na?fa?gósi     'to cause to wash'

And those which bear primary stress:

f.  púgas        'uncooked rice'   mípugas        'abounding in uncooked rice'
    mantíka      'fat'             mímantika      'abounding in fat'
    díŋu         'to leave'        ádiŋgu         'to leave one another'
    paníti       'to strike'       ápaniti        'to strike one another'
    májpi        'hot'             sénmajpi       'very hot'
    agradési     'to give thanks'  sénagradesi    'to give many thanks'

(iii)  Can you suggest a formal reason for the different behaviours of the two types
       of prefix? (NB: the different setting of the End Stress parameter in (f) seems
       to require brute force.)

---

## EXERCISE 6:6  Chamorro Secondary Stress

Following on from the previous exercise, consider the assignment of Chamorro
secondary stresses, "`" (suffixed forms in (a) and stressed prefixed forms in (b)):

a.  swéddu        'salary'              sweddómmu       'your (sg.) salary'
                                        swèddunmáni     'our (excl.) salary'
    inéŋŋulu?      'peeping'            inèŋŋuló?ña      'his peeping'
                                        inèŋŋulu?níha    'their peeping'
    mímantìka     'abounding in fat'    mìmantikóñu      'more abounding in fat'

b.  néŋkanu?      'food'               mínèŋkanu?       'abounding in food'
    adáhi         'be careful'         gófadàhi         'be very careful'
    dómmu?        'to punch'           ádòmmu?          'to punch one another'
    kwentúsi      'to speak to'        ákwentùsi        'to speak to one another'
    úcan          'to rain'            ké?ùcan          'to be about to rain'

(i)   Account for all of these secondary stresses. (Hint: you may want to avail
      yourself of a stress copy rule and a stress deletion rule.)

(ii)  Derive the stress pattern of the words *mímantikɒña, míneŋkanu?, sweddómmu.*

# VII

# Phonological Domains

One of the strongest consequences of the model of Lexical Phonology concerns the linear ordering of affixes, which is supposed to keep pace with their stratal affiliation. In practice, however, many "ordering paradoxes" that contradict this prediction have come to light. Also, it has been shown that affixes do not combine freely within the same stratum, even after semantic and syntactic considerations have been taken account of. These problems, among others, led to a re-evaluation of the model. One interesting and promising development consists in postulating specifically phonological domains which are derived from the grammatical constituents, rather than being identical to them. The need for autonomous phonological domains in postlexical levels has been known for some time. More recently, however, the idea has been extended to the lexical levels. The most commonly accepted phonological domains above the word are the Phonological Phrase, the Intonational Phrase and the Phonological Utterance, each of which can be shown to restrict the scope of some phonological rules in a variety of languages. At word level, the phonological word is not necessarily coextensive with the morphosyntactic word. Below the word, (unnamed) phonological constituents have been proposed which essentially translate morphological constituency without needing to be identical to it, thus providing a way of overcoming some of the difficulties associated with Lexical Phonology in a more elegant and principled manner than some of the earlier remedial proposals (for instance, the "loop"). The availability of phonological domains (often referred to as "prosodic domains" in the literature) also makes it possible to resolve some of the problems posed to syllabification by excess segments, since these segments can now associate to higher constituents, in particular to the phonological word.

## Slave

In the Athapaskan language Slave, spoken in Canada, syllable final consonant contrasts are neutralized to [h], as we see in the alternating forms in (a). Following vowel-initial words prevent neutralization, as we can see in (b):

a.  ts'ah   ~   ts'adé   'hat' (nonpossessed ~ possessed)
    mįh    ~   mįlé    'net'
    dzéeh  ~   dzéegé   'gum'
    téh    ~   tédhé    'cane'

b.  ts'éʔáh          'one eats'
    ts'eʔál íle       'one does not eat'
    ts'eʔál oli       'one is going to eat'

In (c) we show that neutralization does occur word-finally, in spite of the following word being vowel initial:

c.  ohʔáh        enįdhę        's/he wants to eat'
    lsg.opt.eat   3 want

    nénéh        adani         'it is getting long'
    3 is long     3 becomes

    dzéeh        elį           'pink'
    gum          3 is

What is the domain of resyllabification in Slave?

# EXERCISE 7:2 Korean Obstruent Voicing

A process in Korean voices an unaspirated voiceless obstruent when it occurs after a sonorant consonant or a vowel:

a. *Process occurs:*

| | | |
|---|---|---|
| apəci | [abəɟi] | 'father' |
| kɨ cip | [kɨɟip] | 'that house' |
| motɨn kɨlim | [modɨn gɨrim] | 'every picture' |
| suni-ɨj cip | [suniijɟip] | 'Suni's house' |
| kɨ-ka mək-nɨn pap | [kɨga mənnɨn bap] | 'he is eating rice' |
| he-SUB eat-MOD rice | | |
| kɨlim-ɨl pota | [kɨlimɨl boda] | 'look at the picture' |
| picture-ACC see | | |
| kɨ-eke poita | [kɨege boida] | 'show him' |
| he-DAT show | | |
| cap-a pota | [caba boda] | 'try holding' |

b. *Process does not apply:*

| | | |
|---|---|---|
| kæ-ka canta | [kægacanta] | 'the dog is sleeping' |
| dog-NOM sleep | | |
| kæ-ka pap-ɨl məknɨnta | [kægapabɨl mənnɨnda] | 'the dog is eating rice' |
| dog-NOM rice-ACC eat | | |
| ai-eke kwaca-lɨl cunta | [aiegekwaɟarɨl ɟunda] | 'he gives a candy to the child' |
| child-DAT candy-ACC give | | |

Determine the domain of application of the Korean process of obstruent voicing.

# EXERCISE 7:3 Italian Stress Retraction

In standard northern Italian a process of stress retraction to avoid stress clash operates in much the same way as it does in English. We illustrate this in the data in (a) (ˊ = primary stress; ˋ = secondary stress):

a.  metá tórta          →  méta tórta          'half a cake'
    ònoró búdda         →  ónoro búdda         'he honoured Budda'
    si presènterá béne  →  si preséntera béne  'it will be well presented'
    dèlucìderó tútto    →  dèlucídero tútto    '(I) will clarify everything'

Comparing the two sets of sentences in (b) and (c) below, say what is the phonological domain in which stress retraction occurs.

b.  Sára státa ammazzata la vipera                          (< sará státa)
    'The adder has probably been killed'
    Ha gia contato véntitre rágni                           (< ventitré rágni)
    'He has already counted twenty-three spiders'
    Le cítta nórdiche non mi piacciono                      (< cittá nórdiche)
    'I don't like Nordic cities'
    Péschera gránchi almeno, se non aragoste                (< pescherá gránchi)
    'He will fish crabs at least, if not lobsters'

c.  Le cittá mólto nordiche non mi piacciono               (*cítta)
    'I don't like very Nordic cities'
    Pescherá quálque granchio almeno, se non aragoste      (*péschera)
    'He will fish some crab at least, if not lobsters'
    La veritá sálta fuori quasi sempre                     (*vérita)
    'The truth always comes out'

# EXERCISE 7:4  English Sandhi

Consider the following two sandhi phenomena which occur in English:

a.    *v*-Deletion
i.    *give me* some              [gɪmiː]
      *leave them* alone          [liː ðm̩]
      *save them* a seat          [seɪ ðm̩]
      *forgive me* my intrusion   [...gɪː miː]

ii.   *give Maureen* some         *[gɪm...]
      *leave Thelma* alone        *[liː θ...]
      *save those* people a seat  *[seɪ θ...]
      *forgive my* intrusion      *[...gɪː maɪ]

b. **Coronal assimilation**
   Obligatory in:
i. *is Sheila* here?                [ɪ3ʃ...]
   *has Charlotte* arrived?    [hə3ʃ...]
   *was she* there?               [wə3ʃ...]

   Optional in:
ii. *Bo-Peep's sheep*          [...sʃ...]/[...ʃʃ...]
    *Laura's shadow*           [...zʃ...]/[...3ʃ...]

(i)   Do these phenomena affect specific types of word?

(ii)  Can they be accounted for by limiting the processes to particular phonological domains and excluding others?

(iii) Do the facts of English *v*-deletion and coronal assimilation support the postulation of a phonological domain intermediate between the phonological word and the phonological phrase, as proposed in some of the literature?

# EXERCISE 7:5 Tuscan Italian

In the Tuscan dialect of Italian, /k/ becomes [h] within a certain phonological domain, a process known as *Gorgia Toscana*. We list examples below. Say what the phonological domain of application of Gorgia Toscana is.

Hanno [h]atturato sette [h]anguri appena nati
'They have captured seven newly born kangaroos'

I [h]anarini [h]ongolesi [h]ostano molto [h]ari in Ameri[h]a
'Congolese canaries are very expensive in America'

Certe tartarughe, [k]ome si sa, vivono fino a duecento anni
'Certain turtles, as you know, live up to two hundred years'

Almeri[h]o, [k]uando dorme solo, [k]ade spesso dell'ama[h]a
'Almerico, when he sleeps alone, often falls out of the hammock'

# EXERCISE 7:6 The Phonological Word in Hungarian

The two phenomena of vowel harmony and palatalization in Hungarian are confined to the domain of the phonological word. We list below examples of where these processes may and may not take place. To make matters more transparent, we have separated affixes with "-" and words with "#" when there is no break in the spelling. Let us first consider vowel harmony:

a. Vowel Harmony:

| | | |
|---|---|---|
| ölelés | [ølɛle:ʃ] | 'embracement' |
| ölelés-nek | [ølɛle:ʃnɛk] | 'embracement' (dat. sg.) |
| hajó | [hɔjo:] | 'ship' |
| hajó-nak | [hɔjo:nɔk] | 'ship' (dat. sg.) |
| gyerek | [dʲɛrɛk] | 'child' |
| gyerek-ek | [dʲɛrɛkɛk] | 'children' |
| város | [va:roʃ] | 'city' |
| város-ok | [va:roʃok] | 'cities' |
| egyetem-be | [ɛdʲɛtɛmbɛ] | 'to university' |
| iskolá-ba | [iʃkola:bɔ] | 'to school' |

(i) On the basis of the data in (a), state the facts of Hungarian vowel harmony (NB: [i] does not partake of vowel harmony.)

Consider now the following additional forms:

b.

| | | | |
|---|---|---|---|
| be-utaz-ni | [bɛutɔzni] | 'to commute in' | *[bɔutɔzni] |
| fel-ugra-ni | [fɛlugrɔni] | 'to jump up' | *[fɔlugrɔni] |
| oda-men-ni | [odɔmɛnni] | 'to go there' | *[ødɛmɛnni] |
| fö#utca | [fø:uttsɔ] | 'high road' | *[fo:uttsɔ] |
| le#száll | [lɛsa:l] | 'get off' | *[lɔsa:l] |
| le#ül | [lɛyl] | 'sit down' | |
| Buda#pest | [budɔpɛʃt] | 'Budapest' | *[budɔpɔʃt] |
| Buda Pest | | | *[bydɛpɛʃt] |
| könyv#tár | [køɲvta:r] | 'library' | *[køɲvte:r] |
| 'book' 'collection' | | | *[koɲvta:r] |

(ii) On the strength of the evidence from (a) and (b), propose a definition for the Hungarian phonological word.

Now consider palatalization, illustrated in (c):

c.  Palatalization:
    *men-jen*      [mɛɲɲɛn]       'let them go'
    *men-jünk*     [mɛɲɲyŋk]      'let's go'
    *lát-juk*      [laːtʲtʲuk]    'we see something'
    *él-jen*       [eːjjen]       'live (=hooray)!'
    'live' 'long'

Palatalization fails to occur in (d), at least in careful speech:

d.  *én jövök*      [eːnjøvøk]       'I come'
    *fel-jönni*     [fɛljønni]       'to come up'
    *lát járdát*    [laːtjaːrdaːt]   '(s)he sees a pavement'
    *el#jön*        [ɛljøn]          'come away'
    *ön#járó*       [ønjaːroː]       'unmanned vehicle'
    'self' 'goer'
    *véd#jegy*      [veːdjɛdʲ]       'trademark'
    'protection' 'mark'

(iii)  Do the facts of palatalization confirm your proposal on the delimitation of the Hungarian phonological word?

## EXERCISE 7:7  Diyari Stress

The South Australian language Diyari exhibits, in the normal case, the following stress patterns:

a.  *Monomorphemic Words*
    kána              'man'
    ṇánda             'to hit'
    múḷa              'nose'
    wílapìna          'old woman'
    ṇándawàlka        'to close'
    pínadu            'old man'
    púḷuru            'mud'
    mánkaṛa           'girl'
    káṇini            'mother's mother'

b. *Complex words*

| | |
|---|---|
| káṇa-wàra | 'man + PL.' |
| nánda-màli | 'to hit + RECIP.' |
| wíḻapìna-wàra | 'old woman + PL.' |
| ṇándawàlka-tàdi | 'to close + PASS.' |
| táji-jàtimàji | 'to eat + OPT.' |
| káṇa-wàṛa-ṇùndu | 'man + PL. + ABL.' |
| káṇa-ṇi | 'man + LOC.' |
| míndi-na | 'run + PART.' |
| ṇánda-ji | 'hit + PRES.' |
| jáṭa-ji | 'say + PRES.' |
| káṇa-wàṛa-ṇu | 'man + PL. + LOC.' |
| ṇánda-tàri-ji | 'hit + REFL. + PRES.' |

(i) Work out where primary and secondary stresses are located in the cases shown in (a) and (b).

(ii) Suggest how the metrical machinery might assign the correct stresses on these words.

The examples in (c), however, may appear to be problematic for the stress procedure:

c.

| | |
|---|---|
| púḻuru-ṇi | 'mud + LOC.' |
| máda-la-ntu | 'hill + CHARAC. + PROPRIETIVE' |
| púḻuru-ṇi-màṭa | 'mud + LOC. + IDENT.' |
| pínadu-wàṛa | 'old man + PL.' |
| ṇánda-na-màṭa | 'hit + PART. + IDENT.' |
| káṇa-ṇi-màṭa | 'man + LOC. + IDENT.' |
| jákalka-jìrpa-màli-na | 'ask + BEN. + RECIP. + PART.' |

(iii) Explain in what way the data in (c) are problematic.

(iv) Show how the assumption of phonological domains distinct from morphological domains helps to overcome the problem presented in (c)?

EXERCISE **English**
7:8

Divide the collocations below into appropriate Phonological Phrases, Intonational Phrases and Phonological Utterances, giving reasons for the decisions you make:

a.  Perhaps you'd meet me in High Street: it's later than I thought.
b.  The woman I met in the supermarket lives two doors away from you.
c.  Your daughter is clearly very talented.
d.  He told me that your daughter is very talented.
e.  Your daughter, so I hear, is very talented.
f.  John is a writer of pulp fiction.
g.  John is a writer of pulp fiction but a reader of classics.
h.  John is a writer of pulp fiction but a reader of classics and a lover of fine wines.
i.  He has spent many years in Coventry.
j.  Which town has he spent many years in, Coventry or Birmingham?
k.  The party's ove[ɹ]. It's very late.
l.  The party's over. It's very late.
m.  Chris married SARAH, PETER married Jane.
n.  I don't know what to do[w], it's a difficult decision to make.
o.  I don't know what to do. It's time I was leaving.
p.  You'll have to wai[r]. It'll take a little while.
q.  You'll have to wait. It'll spoil otherwise.
r.  Kate's a photographe[ɹ]. Ian's a chemist.
s.  Paul didn't talk to Lucy[j]. I did.
t.  I didn't order a shandy. I ought to have though.

# VIII

# Aspects of Lexical Representation

The autosegmental organization of distinctive features ("Feature Geometry") automatically accounts for a number of apparent violations of the No-Crossing of Lines constraint if in addition we assume that some of the features are unspecified in some segments. This same assumption allows us to circumvent some apparent violations of the Principle of Strict Cyclicity. Moreover, feature underspecification squares up well with the theory of Markedness, of which it can be considered a natural formal expression. In a nutshell, not all segments are lexically specified for all features. Some feature specifications are left out of lexical representation, according to certain theory-specific principles. Under one theory ("Radical Underspecification"), all the valued features that define the default segment in a segment class are not included in the lexicon, and are eventually filled in by redundancy rule to yield a fully specified phonetic form. In another theory ("Contrast-restricted Underspecification"), the determining criterion is surface contrast: only features which are instrumental in the implementation of contrast in a certain context are part of lexical representation. In yet other theories, all or some of the features are monovalent, in such a way that only their presence is materially recorded. Finally, some more phonetically-informed approaches allow for underpecification all the way through to the surface. From whichever standpoint, the formalization of unmarkedness as underspecification has an obvious intuitive appeal, despite which it has not been immune to criticism, and has been rejected in some quarters. There is broad agreement on the basic configuration of the feature geometry, although opinions do diverge on the specifics. One main issue concerns the relationship between vowel and consonant features, some authors strongly favouring identity, while others accept substantially disjoint sets much more readily. On the other hand, there is broad consensus on the existence of feature dependencies and in construing the root of the feature tree as made up of the features [±consonantal, ±sonorant], which are commonly thought not to exhibit independent autosegmental behaviour.

# Lumasaaba

Consider the following data from a dialect of the Bantu language Lumasaaba spoken in Uganda:

| | |
|---|---|
| [iɲɟele] | 'a frog' |
| [xaçele] | 'small frog' |
| [iŋgaːfu] | 'a cow' |
| [xaxaːfu] | 'small cow' |
| [imbeβa] | 'a rat' |
| [xaβeβa] | 'small rat' |
| [iŋgoxo] | 'a hen' |
| [xakoxo] | 'small hen' |
| [iŋgwe] | 'a leopard' |
| [xakwe] | 'small leopard' |
| [indali] | 'a beer' |
| [xatali] | 'small beer' |
| [imboko] | 'a buffalo' |
| [xaβoko] | 'small buffalo' |

(i)   Explain the alternations in each of the stem initial consonants.

(ii)  Propose lexical forms for the consonants.

(iii) Which distinctive features are involved in the derivation of the surface forms?

(iv)  Show the operation of the processes necessary to derive these forms.

## EXERCISE 8:2   Klamath Glottalized Consonants

The Amerindian language Klamath of southwestern Oregon has both glottalized stops and glottalized sonorants, as well as non-glottalized equivalents:

a.   p$^{?}$   t$^{?}$   tʃ$^{?}$   k$^{?}$   q$^{?}$
     p      t      tʃ      k      q
     m$^{?}$   n$^{?}$   w$^{?}$   y$^{?}$   l$^{?}$
     m      n      w      y      l

In word forms, there cannot be two glottalized consonants adjacent, as we show in the examples in (b):

b.   ntʃoq$^{?}$-a              'is deaf'
     ntʃoq-n$^{?}$apg-a         'is almost deaf'
     p$^{?}$et$^{?}$-a          'a hole becomes larger'
     p$^{?}$e-pt$^{?}$-a        'distributive; holes tear out'
     m-p$^{?}$et$^{?}$-a        'makes hole bigger with a round instrument'
     m-p$^{?}$et-k$^{?}$y-o:l-a 'chips open a hole'
     q$^{?}$otʃ$^{?}$-a         'bends'
     q$^{?}$o-qtʃ$^{?}$-a       'distributive; bend'
     n$^{?}$o-k$^{?}$a          'little head'
     n$^{?}$o-n-k$^{?}$a        'distributive; little heads'
     w$^{?}$itʃ$^{?}$-a         'is breathless'
     w$^{?}$i-wtʃ$^{?}$-a       'distributive; is breathless'
     toq$^{?}$-lg-a             'stops an action'
     hos-taq$^{?}$-lg-a         'makes someone stop an action'
     hos-taq-l$^{?}$aq          'make him stop!'
     sno-nt$^{?}$ap$^{?}$-lg-a  'causes to rot down'
     sno-nt$^{?}$ap-l$^{?}$aq-s 'rotted wokas'

(i)   How is the distributive formed in Klamath?

(ii)  Explain the distribution of glottalized consonants.

# EXERCISE 8:3    Koromfe

In the West African language Koromfe a final epenthetic vowel is attached to the
"unmarked" form of the verb (the imperative singular):

a.  baki      'make'          kɔku      'remove leaves'
    digi      'sow'           fɔ̃nɔtu    'rest'
    geri      'rotate'        dɔgsu     'cross'
    ferɪ      'cultivate'     foru      'pound millet'
    bɪrɪ      'mature'        fusu      'move'
    fegeti    'revive'        tullu     'bow'

(i)     List the vowels of Koromfe with their distinctive features.

(ii)    How many manifestations are there of the final epenthetic vowel?

(iii)   Can you suggest what features characterize this vowel?

(iv)    Give a rule to account for the phonetic forms of the vowel.

(v)     What would be the phonetic form of the following verbs?

        dɪŋgV     'have an erection'     dũŋgV     'carry on one's back'
        kerV      'close partially'      dogtV     'cut'
        ganatV    'undo'                 dɔgV      'abandon'

Now consider the data in (b):

b.  babtu     'lie down'      gɛbu      'bang'
    gɛbu      'scrape'        jebu      'chat'
    kɪbtu     'pinch'         hibsu     'fill'
    hẽmsu     'meet'          dubsu     'respect'

(vi)    Can these forms be derived from the rule which you proposed?

(vii)   What is the trigger for their rounding?

(viii)  Revise your rule to account for the data in (b).

# EXERCISE 8:4  Vowel Harmony in Nawuri

The basic vowel system of the Kwa language Nawuri, spoken in Ghana, is as follows:

|   |   |
|---|---|
| i | u |
| ɪ | ʊ |
| e | o |
| ɛ | ɔ |
|  a |

(i)     What are the distinctive features which differentiate these vowels?

In interconsonantal position, underlying short front vowels become central, whether in an open or a closed syllable (this process does not apply to long vowels):

/i, ɪ, e, ɛ/  →  [ɨ, ɨ, ə, ɜ]

Nawuri has a vowel harmony process which affects affixes. This is illustrated by the behaviour of a singular noun class prefix /gV/:

a.     gɨ-baː        'hand'
       gɨ-sɨ-bɨta    'sandal'
       gʊ-sʊ         'ear'
       gʊ-lɔ         'illness'
       gɨ-ɲi         'tooth'
       gɨ-keːliː     'kapok tree'
       gʊ-jo         'yam'
       gʊ-kuː        'digging'

(ii)    What are the underlying features of the prefix vowel?

(iii)   How does it acquire its full specification?

When the initial sound in the stem is /w/, harmony applies as follows:

b.      gʊ-waː      'doing'
         gʊ-wɛː      'sympathy'
         gʊ-wʊrʊː   'hat'

(iv)    Where are the features of the prefix vowel coming from in (b)?

(v)     Show how the vowel harmony process works.

Now consider the following:

c.      gɨ-mu       'heat'
         gɨ-fufuli    'white'
         gɨ-pula     'burial'
         gɨ-boːtoː   'leprosy'
         gɨ-kpo     (type of dance)

(vi)    How is the vowel harmony process failing in (c)?

(vii)   (1)   Why does the prefix vowel in (c) not acquire the feature round?

        (2)   What prevents the spreading of all the features from the stem vowel?

        (3)   Show how spreading is blocked.

(viii)  Does this case shed any light on the rival models of feature geometry presented in chapter 17 of *A Course in Phonology*?

## EXERCISE Ainu
## 8:5

Ainu is a language of indeterminate origin formerly spoken in the island of Hokkaidō (in northern Japan) and the Sakhalin and Kurile islands (under Russian administration). In this language, the identity of the transitivizing vowel suffix depends on the features of the root vowel. However, the language possesses two classes of root, determined by the behaviour of the suffix. These two classes are illustrated in (a) and (b) respectively:

a.  mak-a    'to open'      tas-a    'to cross'
    ker-e    'to touch'     per-e    'to tear'
    pis-i    'to ask'       nik-i    'to fold'
    pop-o    'to boil'      tom-o    'to concentrate'
    tus-u    'to shake'     yup-u    'to tighten'

b.  hum-i    'to chop up'   mus-i    'to choke'
    pok-i    'to lower'     hop-i    'to leave behind'
    pir-u    'to wipe'      kir-u    'to alter'
    ket-u    'to rub'       rek-u    'to ring'

If the verb belongs to the (b) class but the root vowel is low, the selection of the suffix vowel is lexically determined (listed in the lexicon with the root):

c.  kar-i    'to rotate'    sar-i    'to look back'
    ram-u    'to think'     rap-u    'to flutter'

(i)    List the vowels of Ainu with their relevant features.

(ii)   How is the suffix vowel determined in the class of verbs listed in (a)?

(iii)  How is the suffix vowel determined in the class of verbs listed in (b)?

(iv)   Can the OCP be brought in to account for the different behaviour of both sets of suffix vowels?

# EXERCISE 8:6 Ngbaka

Like Ainu in exercise 8:5 above, the Congo-Kordofanian language Ngbaka has two types of (monomorphemic) disyllabic word, as we show in (a) and (b) below:

a.
| liki | 'to heat' | tulu | 'mushroom' |
|------|-----------|------|------------|
| ʔele | 'to forget' | zoko | 'beautiful' |
| bɛnɛ | 'to cement' | bɔŋɔ | 'brain' |

b.
| niɲɛ | 'amusement' | gbie | 'field' |
|------|-------------|------|---------|
| seti | 'lying down' | sɛti | 'luck' |
| kɔpu | 'tumbler' | pɛpu | 'wind' |

The vowel combinations in (c) cannot occur in Ngbaka words:

c.
| *i...u | *u...i | *e...ɛ | *ɛ...e | *o...ɔ | *ɔ...o | | |
|--------|--------|--------|--------|--------|--------|--------|--------|
| *e...o | *o...e | *ɛ...ɔ | *ɔ...ɛ | *e...ɔ | *ɔ...e | *ɛ...o | *o...ɛ |

(i) How are vowel combinations restricted in Ngbaka?

Also like Ainu, the vowel /a/ seems to be exempt from the restrictions demonstrated in (a), (b) and (c) above:

d.
| nzambu | 'palm nut pulp' | kema | 'monkey' |
|--------|----------------|------|----------|
| dalɛ | 'Acacia silvicola' | kɔla | 'paternal aunt' |
| zimba | 'to look for' | kola | 'debt' |

(ii) List the vowels of Ngbaka with their relevant feature specifications.

(iii) Account for the distribution of vowels in (a).

(iv) Account for the prohibitions in (c).

(v) Suggest why the forms in (d) are unaffected by either restriction.

# EXERCISE Polish Nasal Vowels
## 8:7

Polish has two "nasal vowels", orthographically *ą* and *ę*. The label is misleading, however, because they do not surface as nasal, but as a sequence of an oral vowel and a nasal segment (the diacritic "´" indicates a prepalatal articulation, and therefore the symbol [ć] stands for a voiceless prepalatal affricate, IPA [ɕ]; we include the orthographic representations in italics for the benefit of readers with a knowledge of Polish):

a.
| | | |
|---|---|---|
| *ząb* | [zomp] | 'tooth' |
| *zęby* | [zembi] | 'teeth' |
| *rządu* | [ʒondu] | 'government' |
| *zajęty* | [zajentɨ] | 'busy' (masc. sg.) |
| *ręce* | [rentse] | 'hands' |
| *tęcza* | [tentʃa] | 'rainbow' |
| *bądź* | [bońć] | 'be' (imperative) |
| *zajęci* | [zajeńći] | 'busy' (masc. pers. pl.) |
| *węgiel* | [veŋgʲel] | 'coal' |

b.
| | | |
|---|---|---|
| *mąż* | [mõwʃ] | 'husband' |
| *wąski* | [võwski] | 'narrow' (masc. sg.) |
| *męski* | [mẽwski] | 'man's' (masc. sg.) |
| *książka* | [kśõwʃka] | 'book' |
| *gęsi* | [gʲẽwśi] | 'geese' |
| *węch* | [vẽwx] | 'smell' |
| *dążyć* | [dõwʒić] | 'aspire' |
| *rzęsa* | [ʒẽwsa] | 'eyelash' |

(i)    In what way does the behaviour of the two "nasal vowels" differ in the data blocks in (a) and (b)?

(ii)   What would be the best lexical representation for the nasality in question?

(iii)  What determines the identity of the nasal consonants in (a)?

(iv)   Assuming (with Padgett 1994) that [w] is assigned as default in the absence of a specified place of articulation, give rules to show how the phonetic forms in (b) are attained.

# EXERCISE 8:8   Capanhua

Consider the following data from the Panoan language Capanhua, spoken in South America:

a.    /tsiponki/       [tsipõnki]       'down river'
       /wiran-ai/      [wirãnai]       'I pushed it'
       /hama-wi/      [h̃ãmawi]      'walk below'
       /hama-ʔona/    [h̃ãmãʔõna]    'walking towards'
       /bimi/          [bĩmi]         'fruit'

b.    /waran/         [warã]         'squash'
       /pojan/         [põjã]          'arm'
       /bawin/        [bãw̃ĩ]        'catfish'

(i)      What type of sound is subject to nasalization?

(ii)     How is this nasalization process triggered?

(iii)    What is the direction of the process?

(iv)    Using autosegmental formalization, show the spreading process.

(v)      What is the surface difference between the triggering sound in (a) and in (b)?

(vi)    How will the forms [bõõ] 'hair' and [bãnawi] 'plant it' be derived?

Now consider the further set of data in (c):

c.    /wiran-wi/            [wirãw̃ĩ]           'push it'
       /wiran-jasaʔaʔn-wi/   [wirãjãʃãʔãʔw̃ĩ]   'push it sometime'

(vii)   In what way is the process in (c) different from or similar to that demonstrated in (a) and (b)?

# EXERCISE 8:9  Kikongo Nasal Harmony

In the Bantu language Kikongo, spoken in the southwestern region of the Democratic Republic of Congo, the consonants of the perfective active suffix *-idi* and the perfective passive suffix *-ulu* become nasal if the verb stem contains a nasal consonant:

a.
| | |
|---|---|
| m-bud-idi | 'I hit' |
| m-bul-ulu | 'I was hit' |
| n-suk-idi | 'I washed' |
| n-suk-ulu | 'I was washed' |
| tu-kun-ini | 'we planted' |
| masaŋgu ma-kin-unu | 'the maize was planted' |
| tu-nik-ini | 'we ground' |
| masaŋgu ma-nik-unu | 'the maize was ground' |

(i)  Show how the process operates formally.

Now compare the following sets of data in (b), where nasal harmony fails to apply, and in (c), where it applies as we might anticipate:

b.
| | |
|---|---|
| tu-biŋg-idi | 'we hunted' |
| tu-biŋg-ulu | 'we were hunted' |
| tu-koŋg-idi | 'we tied' |
| tu-koŋg-ulu | 'we were tied' |

c.
| | |
|---|---|
| tu-meŋg-ini | 'we hated' |
| tu-meŋg-ono | 'we were hated' |
| tu-mant-ini | 'we climbed' |
| wu-mant-unu | 'it was climbed' |

(ii)  Offer an explanation as to why the forms in (b) do not undergo nasal harmony.

(iii)  Can the assumption of underspecification help? (Hint: the only consonant clusters allowed in Kikongo are homorganic nasal plus stop clusters.)

(iv)  Why does nasal harmony apply in the data in (c)?

# EXERCISE 8:10 Reduplication in Feʔ Feʔ Bamileke

Reduplication in the Bantu language Feʔ Feʔ Bamileke, spoken in Cameroon, takes the form of a CV prefix, where the melody for the C is copied from the stem. A number of factors affect the choice of vowel which will occur in the reduplicated prefix. Consider the following data sets:

a.    High root vowel:

| | | | |
|---|---|---|---|
| si-sii | 'to spoil' | pi-pii | 'to get' |
| su-su | 'to vomit' | ku-kuu | 'to carve' |

(i)    Give a formal account of the reduplicative prefixation.

b.    In some roots with nonhigh vowels, the reduplicant vowel is partially identifiable with the base vowel:

| | | | |
|---|---|---|---|
| ji-jee | 'to see' | ti-tee | 'to remove' |
| ci-cen | 'to moan' | ti-ten | 'to stand' |
| ci-cæʔ | 'to trample' | ti-tæʔ | 'to bargain' |
| mu-mo | 'to kill time' | ku-ko | 'to take' |
| pu-poh | 'to be afraid' | ku-koh | 'to be small' |

(ii)    Give a formal account of the relationship between both vowels.

c.    In other roots with nonhigh vowels, there is no relation between the base vowel and the reduplicant vowel:

| | | | |
|---|---|---|---|
| pɨ-pee | 'to hate' | kɨ-kee | 'to refuse' |
| pɨ-pen | 'to accept' | ɣɨ-ɣen | 'to go' |
| pɨ-pæʔ | 'to commit suicide' | kɨ-kæʔ | 'to fry' |
| tɨ-to | 'to punch' | cɨ-co | 'to fall' |
| tɨ-toh | 'to pass' | zɨ-za | 'to eat' |

(iii)   Is the relation in feature content between the consonant and the vowel in the base the same in (b) and (c)? (NB: you have to remember that not all theories of distinctive features contain the same set of features.)

(iv)   Can you relate the different behaviour of the reduplicant vowel to the relation it bears to the consonant and vowel in the base?

# IX

# Derivational Theory

In the classical model of generative phonology the lexical level of representation is mapped onto the surface level by means of a set of ordered rules which apply in a sequence, in a manner known as a derivation. The ordering of the rules is crucial to the procedure, since a different ordering will obviously yield a different output. Some rules attain the desired ordering if they are allowed to apply freely, and are said to be "internally ordered". When this is not the case, rules must be "externally ordered", that is, their ordering needs to be stipulated. With regard to their mutual effect, rules can stand in a "feeding" or a "bleeding" order. A feeding order implies that the application of the first rule effects a change in the input that makes the application of the second rule possible. By contrast, in a bleeding order the first rule destroys the input that the second rule requires. If we invert a feeding order we obtain a "counterfeeding" order, and if we invert a bleeding order we get a "counterbleeding" order. When the application of a rule has no effect on the application of another rule, we say that the two rules are "non-interacting". The interaction between rules can lend rule systems remarkable levels of complexity. The order of the rules is established on empirical grounds in the first place, and by the logical principle of transitivity in the absence of empirical evidence. In addition to elucidating their ordering, rules need to be labelled as cyclic or noncyclic, and be allotted to lexical (or postlexical) strata.

**Sea Dayak**

Consider the interaction of two rules in the Western Malayo-Polynesian language Sea Dayak:

a.   Nasalization: The feature [+nasal] spreads rightwards from a nasal consonant to all nuclear vowels, its progress being halted by the presence of a "true" consonant.

      mãta     'an eye'
      gonẽ     'a sack'
      mõã     'the face'
      mãjã     'a season'

b.   Cluster simplification: Voiced stops and affricates are deleted after a nasal.

      /naŋgaʔ/ → nãŋa     'straighten'

The interaction of these two rules results in minimal pairs of the following type:

c.   nãŋãʔ     'set up a ladder'     *vs.*
     nãŋaʔ     'straighten'

(i)   What are the underlying representations of the forms in (c)?

(ii)  What is the relationship between rules (a) and (b)?

(iii) Demonstrate this relationship.

# EXERCISE 9:2 Tunica

In the Penutian language Tunica, formerly spoken around the Gulf of Mexico, the vowel /a/ assimilates to the backness and roundness of a preceding vowel if, either the two vowels are adjacent, or are separated only by a glottal stop:

a.

| Infinitive | 3rd sg. masc. | 3rd sg. fem. | 3rd sg. fem. pres. prog. | |
|---|---|---|---|---|
| pó | pópuhki | pópɔki | póhkpaki | 'look' |
| pí | pípuhki | pípɛki | píhkpaki | 'emerge' |
| já | jápuhki | jápaki | jáhkpaki | 'do' |
| ʧú | ʧúpuhki | ʧúpɔki | ʧúhkpaki | 'take' |

Another rule of the language deletes an unstressed vowel before a glottal stop, the result of which can be seen in (b):

b.

| Infinitive | 3rd sg. masc. | 3rd sg. fem. | 3rd sg. fem. pres. prog. | |
|---|---|---|---|---|
| hára | hárpuhki | hárpaki | hárahkpáki | 'sing' |
| hípu | híppuhki | híppɔki | hípuhkpáki | 'dance' |
| náʃi | náʃpuhki | náʃpɛki | náʃihkpáki | 'lead someone' |

(i) Explain how the application of the two rules derives the 3rd sg. fem. forms [hípʔɔki] and [náʃʔɛki].

(ii) What is the ordering relationship between these two rules?

# EXERCISE 9:3 Shona

In the Central Bantu language, Shona, spoken in Zimbabwe, there is a rule of nasal assimilation and another which causes postnasal voiceless stops /p t k/ to lose their oral place and become [h]. Examples illustrating the results of these processes are shown below (high tones are marked with an acute accent):

| | | | |
|---|---|---|---|
| ku-p-a | 'to give' | m-h-a | 'give it to me' |
| agá-ka | 'little cow' | íŋ-ha | 'cow' |
| uru-toki | 'finger' | in-hoki | 'fingers' |

How must these two rules be applied in order to yield the desired results?

# EXERCISE 9:4 Rule Interaction in Korean

In the Kyungsang dialect of Korean the presence of the vowel /i/ causes a process of "umlaut", that is, harmonization in frontness of the vowel of the preceding syllable. Since Korean has no rounded front vowels in its inventory, this causes rounded back vowels to become unrounded front ones (this is reminiscent of the English *goose~geese* alternations we discuss in chapter 6 of *A Course in Phonology*). Umlaut occurs across non-coronal and anterior coronal consonants. A further process triggered by /i/ is the palatalization of preceding [+anterior] consonants, like [s], [n] and [l]. The data in (a) illustrate the situation (the voiced~voiceless stop and /l/~/r/ alternations observable in the data are irrelevant to this exercise):

a.  | /koki/ | [kegi] | 'meat' |
    | /mǝk+hi+ta/ | [mekʰida] | 'to be eaten' |
    | /cuk+i+ta/ | [cigida] | 'to kill' |
    | /api/ | [æbi] | 'father' |
    | /sum+ki+ta/ | [ʃimgida] | 'to hide' |
    | /k'ini/ | [k'iɲi] | 'meal' |
    | /ses+i/ | [seʃi] | 'three' (subject) |
    | /kɨli+ta/ | [kirida] | 'to draw, paint' |
    | /puti/ | [pidi] | 'by all means' |

(i)   Formalize the rules of umlaut and palatalization and show how they interact.

As we show in (b), the umlaut process is blocked by palatal ([−anterior]) consonants, which Hume (1990) formalizes as having [-anterior] linked via [coronal] to the V-place node (this feature model is discussed in section 11 of chapter 17 of *A Course in Phonology*):

b.  | /kacʰi/ | [kacʰi] | *[kæcʰi] | 'value' |
    | /toci+ta/ | [toɟida] | *[teɟida] | 'worsening of an illness' |
    | /huci+ta/ | [huɟida] | *[hiɟida] | 'to be old-fashioned' |

(ii)  Why should umlaut be blocked by [-anterior] consonants?

The examples in (c) show that umlaut is also blocked by derived palatals:

c.  | /kasi/ | [kaʃi] | *[kæʃi] | 'thorn' |
    | /ǝps+i/ | [ǝpʃi] | *[epʃi] | 'without' |
    | /ǝmǝni/ | [ǝmǝɲi] | *[ǝmeɲi] | 'mother' |
    | /tani+ta/ | [taɲida] | *[tæɲida] | 'to travel/commute' |
    | /p'al+li/ | [p'aʎʎi] | *[p'æʎʎi] | 'fast' |

(iii) In what way does the evidence in (c) contradict that in (a) with regard to the ordering of the rules of umlaut and palatalization? Give a formal demonstration of the ordering paradox.

(iv)   Make a proposal to get the umlaut situation right in all of (a), (b) and (c).
Hint: Hume (1990) gives the following relevant information, e.g. [seʃi] (in (a))
and *[kæʃi] (in (c)):

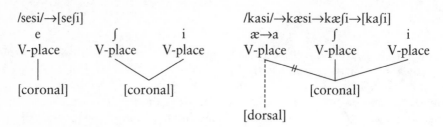

(v)    List the three rules that participate in the derivation and specify their ordering.

(vi)   Give the derivation of [seʃi], [kacʰi] and [kaʃi].

## EXERCISE 9:5   Lumasaaba

Consider the following data, some of which featured in exercise 8:1, from three
dialects of Lumasaaba, a language spoken in Uganda. Assuming that all the dialects
are derived from the same base form, answer the questions below, supplying a clear
explanation of your answers.

I   NOUNS

| A | B | C | |
|---|---|---|---|
| [iɲɟele] | [iɲcele] | [iːcele] | 'a frog' |
| [xaçele] | [kacele] | [kacele] | 'small frog' |
| [iŋgaːfu] | [iɲkaːfu] | [iːkaːfu] | 'a cow' |
| [xaxaːfu] | [kakaːfu] | [kakaːfu] | 'small cow' |
| [imbeβa] | [imbeβa] | [imbeβa] | 'a rat' |
| [xaβeβa] | [kaβeβa] | [kaβeβa] | 'small rat' |
| [iŋgoxo] | [iŋgoko] | [iŋgoko] | 'a hen' |
| [xakoxo] | [kagoko] | [kagoko] | 'small hen' |
| [iŋgwe] | [iŋgwe] | [iŋgwe] | 'a leopard' |
| [xakwe] | [kagwe] | [kagwe] | 'small leopard' |
| [indali] | [indali] | [indali] | 'a beer' |
| [xatali] | [kadali] | [kadali] | 'small beer' |
| [imboko] | [imbogo] | [imbogo] | 'a buffalo' |
| [xaβoko] | [kaβogo] | [kaβogo] | 'small buffalo' |

(i)     How many manifestations of the two prefixes can you identify?

(ii)    Suggest what the common base form for each of these two prefixes might be.

(iii)   List the base forms of the seven stem morphemes.

(iv)    A number of phonological processes apply. Using all the appropriate machinery available, write rules which describe these processes and indicate which of the rules apply to which dialect(s).

(v)     Produce a mini-grammar for each of the dialects, indicating the ordering of rules where applicable.

## II   VERBS

(vi)    To what extent are the processes which apply to nouns also applicable in the case of the verbs listed below? Extend your grammars to include these verbal forms.

| A | B | C | |
|---|---|---|---|
| [xuçina] | [kucina] | [kucina] | 'to dance' |
| [iɲɟina] | [iɲcina] | [iːcina] | 'I dance' |
| [xudima] | [kudima] | [kudima] | 'to run' |
| [indima] | [indima] | [indima] | 'I run' |
| [xulima] | [kulima] | [kulima] | 'to dig' |
| [inima] | [inima] | [inima] | 'I dig' |
| [xupululuxa] | [kubululuka] | [kubululuka] | 'to fly' |
| [imbululuxa] | [imbululuka] | [imbululuka] | 'I fly' |
| [xujoːla] | [kujoːla] | [kujoːla] | 'to grow' |
| [iɲɟoːla] | [iɲɟoːla] | [iɲɟoːla] | 'I grow' |
| [xutsowa] | [kudzoha] | [kuzowa] | 'to pound' |
| [iːtsowa] | [indzoha] | [inzowa] | 'I pound' |
| [xuβona] | [kuβona] | [kuβona] | 'to see' |
| [imona] | [imona] | [imona] | 'I see' |
| [xuwamba] | [kuhamba] | [kuhamba] | 'to hold' |
| [imbamba] | [impamba] | [iːpamba] | 'I hold' |
| [xuramba] | [kutamba] | [kutamba] | 'to act' |
| [indamba] | [intamba] | [iːtamba] | 'I act' |

# EXERCISE 9:6 Yawelmani Vowel System

The data below come from the Yawelmani dialect of Yokuts, an American Indian language of California. Yawelmani has the following sets of long and short vowels (short [e] is a predictable variant of underlying [eː]):

| Short | | Long | |
|---|---|---|---|
| i | u | | |
| (e) | o | eː | oː |
| | a | | aː |

Each of the suffixes exemplified below has two variants:

a.

| future passive | passive aorist | precative gerundial | dubitative | |
|---|---|---|---|---|
| xil-nit | xil-it | xil-ʔas | xil-al | 'tangle' |
| hud-nut | hud-ut | hud-ʔas | hud-al | 'recognize' |
| gop-nit | gop-it | gop-ʔos | gop-ol | 'take care of' |
| max-nit | max-it | max-ʔas | max-al | 'procure' |

(i)    What causes the choice of suffix variant?

In (b) we show verb stems with two suffixes:

b.

| | max-sit-hin | 'procure' (indirect, nonfuture) |
|---|---|---|
| | koʔ-sit-hin | 'throw' (indirect, nonfuture) |
| | tul-sut-hun | 'burn' (indirect, nonfuture) |
| | bok-sit-ka | 'find' (indirect, imperative) |
| (cf. | bok-ko | 'find' (imperative)) |

(ii)    Give a formal account of the suffix variants.

The data in (c) show a length alternation in the stem:

c.

| future passive | passive aorist | precative gerundial | dubitative | |
|---|---|---|---|---|
| mek-nit | meːk-it | mek-ʔas | meːk-al | 'swallow' |
| sog-nut | soːg-ut | sog-ʔas | soːg-al | 'unwrap' |
| dos-nit | doːs-it | dos-ʔos | doːs-ol | 'report' |
| tan-nit | taːn-it | tan-ʔas | taːn-al | 'go' |

(iii)    What are the underlying forms of these verb stems?

(iv)     Account formally for the alternating vowel length in the stems.

The verbs in (d) exhibit an alternation between epenthetic [i] and Ø:

d.
| *future* | *dubitative* | *gerundive* | *nonfuture* | |
|----------|--------------|-------------|-------------|-----|
| paʔt-en  | paʔt-al      | paʔit-mi    | paʔit-hin   | 'fight' |
| lihm-en  | lihm-al      | lihim-mi    | lihim-hin   | 'run' |
| logw-en  | logw-ol      | logiw-mi    | logiw-hin   | 'pulverize' |
| ʔugn-on  | ʔugn-al      | ʔugun-mu    | ʔugun-hun   | 'drink' |

(v)      Give an explanation for the rule of epenthesis.

(vi)     How does the epenthesis process interact with the first rule you proposed?

Now consider the forms in (e):

e.
| *dubitative* | *gerundive/*<br>*nonfuture* | |
|--------------|--------------|------------------------|
| sonl-ol      | soːnil-mi    | 'put on the back' |
| ʔaml-al      | ʔaːmil-hin   | 'help' |
| mojn-ol      | moːjin-mi    | 'get tired' |
| salk-al      | saːlik-hin   | 'wake up' |

(vii)    From the evidence in (e) say what the ordering of the three rules is.

(viii)   Give derivations for [soːnil-hin], [mojn-al] and [dos-ʔos].

# X

# Optimality Theory

A recent version of generative phonology, "Optimality Theory", departs from the model described in the previous section in important ways. In particular, OT dispenses with overt rules, and controls surface forms by means of violable constraints. In a nutshell, the model is as follows. Lexical representations are postulated along the same lines as in classical generative phonology. Rather than being acted upon by specific ordered rules, however, these forms are freely processed into an open number of "candidates". Each set of candidates is then evaluated by a set of ranked violable constraints: the candidate that best complies with the higher ranked constraints wins, and is selected as the surface form. The constraints cluster in families on grounds of substance and function: faithfulness constraints (imposing likeness of the output to the input), markedness constraints (favouring unmarked elements), structural constraints (shaping inputs into canonical forms), alignment constraints (regulating linear arrangements of segments and forms), correspondence constraints (favouring sameness), and so on. The substance of the constraints is assumed to be universal, part of the general language endowment. The language-specific phonology is thus reduced to the ranking of the constraints, which varies from language to language. The learner's task consists of learning the constraint rankings and the underlying forms. More recent developments in Optimality Theory favour correspondence relations between surface forms, and some even allow for lexical allomorphy. Optimality Theory can also be used to regulate morphological processes, and the interaction between morphology and phonology.

# A Child's Language

The examples below are the pronunciations of a 2-year-old child acquiring language in a monolingual American English-speaking household

| | |
|---|---|
| [kin] | 'clean' |
| [dɔ] | 'draw' |
| [piz] | 'please' |
| [fɛn] | 'friend' |
| [gaɪ] | 'sky' |
| [bɪw] | 'spill' |
| [dɔ] | 'straw' |
| [gɪn] | 'skin' |
| [bun] | 'spoon' |
| [dɑː] | 'star' |
| [so] | 'snow' |
| [sʊki] | 'snookie' |
| [sɪp] | 'slip' |
| [sip] | 'sleep' |

Assuming a correspondence relationship between the adult output and the child's output, work out a set of constraints which will ensure that the optimal output prevails in the light of the undominated *COMPLEX. In order to determine the child's choice of surviving consonant, you should bear in mind that onset consonants are not moraic, and therefore incur a violation of a constraint in the set:

μ/Y: Each Y must be parsed as a mora
(where Y represents a sound or group of sounds)

Ranking of such constraints is in accordance with the sonority scale (μ/a ≫ μ/i, u ≫ μ/r etc.), and takes into consideration that lower sonority onsets are to be preferred over higher sonority ones.

# EXERCISE 10:2 Pali Syllables

In this exercise we repeat the data you were asked to analyse in exercise 3:4 above. Bearing in mind the possible types of relationship between Faithfulness and Markedness, the specific task we are asking you to perform is to investigate the historical evolution of Sanskrit, the parent language, into Pali, the language of the Theravādin Buddhist canon, and to offer an Optimality-theoretic account of the evolution of syllabification in Pali:

a. *Sanskrit*     b. *Pali*

i.
| | | |
|---|---|---|
| tatas | tato | 'therefrom' |
| punar | puno, puna | 'again' |
| praːpatat | papata | 'hurled down' |

ii.
| | | |
|---|---|---|
| danta | danta | 'tamed' |
| sambudd<sup>h</sup>a | sambudd<sup>h</sup>a | 'enlightened' |
| sakt<sup>h</sup>i | satt<sup>h</sup>i | 'thigh' |
| mudga | mugga | 'bean' |
| śabda | sadda | 'words' |
| b<sup>h</sup>akta | b<sup>h</sup>atta | 'rice' |
| sapta | satta | 'seven' |
| karka | kakka | 'a precious stone' |
| sarpa | sappa | 'snake' |
| valka | vakka | 'the bark of a tree' |
| d<sup>h</sup>arma | d<sup>h</sup>amma | 'righteousness' |
| karṇa | kaṇṇa | 'ear' |
| kalmaṣa | kammasa | 'spotted' |
| karṣaka | kassaka | 'farmer' |

iii.
| | | |
|---|---|---|
| traana | taana | 'protection' |
| kramati | kamati | 'walks' |
| prati | paṭi | 'against' |
| śvaśru | sassu | 'mother-in-law' |

(i)   On the assumption of common underlying representations for the two languages during the period of evolution, postulate constraint rankings which will account for columns (a) and (b) in each of the data sets (i, ii, and iii) individually.

(ii)  Give the combined ranking for the three sets. (Hint: You will need to include a CODA CONDITION constraint in the set for consideration.)

# EXERCISE Malay Syllable Structure
# 10:3

Consider the sets of data in (a) and (b) below, from the Austronesian language Bahasa Melayu/Indonesia as spoken in Malaysia. On the basis of these data, suggest what the restrictions on syllabification are in this language (ignore any other results of segmental processes):

a.  *English loanwords*

|  |  |
| --- | --- |
| stamp | [sətem] |
| glass | [gəlas] |
| class | [kəlas] |
| club | [kəlap] |
| post | [pos] |

b.  *Prefixed forms*

|  |  |  |
| --- | --- | --- |
| /di+ubah/ | [diʔubah] | 'to move' (passive) |
| /di+ikat/ | [diʔikat] | 'to tie' (passive) |
| /dʒuru+atʃara/ | [dʒuruʔatʃarə] | 'master of ceremonies' |
| /sə+indah/ | [səʔindah] | 'to be beautiful as' |
| /sə+elok/ | [səʔeloʔ] | 'to be pretty as' |

Give the appropriate ranking for the constraints MAX-IO, DEP-IO, NO-CODA, ONSET and *COMPLEX, in order to yield the correct forms.

# EXERCISE Lenakel Syllabification
# 10:4

The data below are repeated from exercise 3:2, where you were asked to determine the shape of the possible syllable in the Austronesian language Lenakel, from the position of epenthetic vowels.

a.  *Word Initial*

|  |  |  |
| --- | --- | --- |
| /t-n-ak-ol/ | [tɨnágɔl] | 'you (sg.) will do it' |
| /t-r-ep-ol/ | [tɨrébɔl] | 'he will then do it' |
| /n-n-ol/ | [nínɔl] | 'you (sg.) have done it' |
| /r-n-ol/ | [rínɔl] | 'he has done it' |

b.  *Word Medial*
    /kam-n-m̃an-n/      [kàmnɨmánɨn]      'for her brother'
    /əs-ət-pn-aan/       [əsɨdbənán]       'don't go up there'
    /k-ar-(ə)pkom/      [karbə́gɔm]       'they are heavy'

c.  *Word Final*
    /əpk-əpk/            [əbgə́bək]        'to be pregnant'
    /apn-apn/            [abnábən]        'free'
    /ark-ark/            [argárɨkʰ]       'to growl'
    /r-əm-əŋn/          [rɨmə́ŋən]        'he was afraid'
    /n-əm-əpk/          [nɨmə́bəkʰ]       'you (sg.) took it'

(i)   Work out the constraints and their rankings to ensure victory to the correct candidate.

(ii)  We pointed out in exercise 3:2 that there are two potential epenthesis sites in words like /əpk-əpk/ → [əbgə́bək], neither of which would violate the syllable structure constraints of the language. Suggest which constraint should be taken into consideration in order to ensure that the correct site is chosen.

# EXERCISE 10:5  Polish Onsets

Assuming the Polish onset to be maximally binary, give a list of ranked constraints which will account for the examples listed below (the symbol [ć] stands for a prepalatal affricate and [ś] stands for a prepalatal fricative: IPA [tɕ] and [ɕ], respectively):

| | | | |
|---|---|---|---|
| [fść]iekly | 'furious' | [bzd]ura | 'nonsense' |
| [pʃtʃ]ola | 'bee' | [fsp]anialy | 'great' |
| [fst]yd | 'shame' | [gʒb]iet | 'back' |
| [lśn]ić | 'shine' | [lgn]ąć | 'to stick' |
| [mdl]ić | 'to feel seasick' | [mść]ić się | 'avenge' |

(Hint: bear in mind that segments need not be licensed by the syllable node.)

# EXERCISE 10:6 Pintupi Stress

In exercise 4:3 you worked out the stress algorithm settings which would account for the Pama-Nyungan language Pintupi, from Australia. We repeat the data below:

| | |
|---|---|
| páɳa | 'earth' |
| tʲúʈaya | 'many' |
| máɭawàna | 'through from behind' |
| púɭiŋkàlatʲu | 'we (sat) on the hill' |
| tʲámulùmpatʲùŋku | 'our relation' |
| ʈíɭirìɳulàmpatʲu | 'the fire for our benefit flared up' |
| kúranʲùluìmpatʲùɻa | 'the first one (who is) our relation' |
| yúmaɻiŋkamàratʲùɻaka | 'because of mother-in-law' |

Work out the appropriate constraints and their rankings to yield the stress pattern for Pintupi. Take into consideration constraints in the ALIGN family, as well as possibly NONFIN and FOOT-BIN.

# EXERCISE 10:7 Garawa Stress

The data below come from the Australian language Garawa. We have marked stresses and foot boundaries, but have not indicated the location of the primary stress, as it is irrelevant to this exercise.

| | |
|---|---|
| (yámi) | 'eye' |
| (púnja)la | 'white' |
| (wátjim)(páɳu) | 'armpit' |
| (káma)la(řinji) | 'wrist' |
| (yáka)(láka)(lámpa) | 'loose' |
| (ŋánki)ři(kírim)(páyi) | 'fought with boomerangs' |
| (ŋámpa)(láɲin)(múkun)(jína) | 'at our many' |
| (náři)ŋin(múkkun)(jína)(mířa) | 'at our own many' |
| (nímpa)(láɲin)(múku)(nánji)(mířa) | 'from our own two' |

Availing yourself of the set of Alignment and foot-form constraints and any others which may be applicable, work out the ranking which will yield the stress pattern of Garawa.

# EXERCISE 10:8 Diyari Stress Again

Exercise 7:7 called on phonological domains in order to derive the foot structure of the Australian language Diyari. We repeat the data set below:

a. *Monomorphemic words*

| | |
|---|---|
| kána | 'man' |
| nánda | 'to hit' |
| múḷa | 'nose' |
| wíḷapína | 'old woman' |
| ŋándawálka | 'to close' |
| pínadu | 'old man' |
| púḷuru | 'mud' |
| mánkaṛa | 'girl' |
| káṇini | 'mother's mother' |

b. *Complex words*

| | |
|---|---|
| káṇa-wára | 'man + PL.' |
| ṇánda-máli | 'to hit + RECIP.' |
| wíḷapìna-wára | 'old woman + PL.' |
| ŋándawálka-tádi | 'to close + PASS.' |
| táji-játimáji | 'to eat + OPT.' |
| káṇa-wáṛa-ŋúndu | 'man + PL. + ABL.' |
| káṇa-ṇi | 'man + LOC.' |
| míndi-na | 'run + PART.' |
| ṇánda-ji | 'hit + PRES.' |
| jáṭa-ji | 'say + PRES.' |
| káṇa-wáṛa-ŋu | 'man + PL. + LOC.' |
| nánda-tári-ji | 'hit + REFL. + PRES.' |
| púḷuru-ṇi | 'mud + LOC.' |
| máda-la-ntu | 'hill + CHARAC. + PROPRIETIVE' |
| púḷuru-ṇi-máṭa | 'mud + LOC. + IDENT.' |
| pínadu-wáṛa | 'old man + PL.' |
| ṇánda-na-máṭa | 'hit + PART. + IDENT.' |
| káṇa-ṇi-máṭa | 'man + LOC. + IDENT.' |
| jákalka-jírpa-máli-na | 'ask + BEN. + RECIP. + PART.' |

The following constraints, properly ranked, should allow you to account for the correct foot structure for Diyari:

| Ft-Bin: | Feet are binary |
|---|---|
| FtType$_{TROCH}$: | Feet are trochaic |
| Align-Morpheme: | Align(Morpheme, Left, PrWd, Left) |
| | Align(Morpheme, Right, PrWd, Right) |
| Parse-Syll: | Every syllable belongs to a foot |
| All-Ft-L: | Align (Foot, Left, PrWd, Left) |
| | (All feet are aligned with the left edge of the prosodic word) |

# EXERCISE 10:9   Syllable Weight and Syllable Count in Huave Loanwords

The Penutian language Huave spoken in Oaxaca, Mexico, contains large numbers of loans from Spanish. The result of the nativization of these Spanish words can be manifested in a number of different ways. In Huave, stress falls on the final syllable if it is heavy, otherwise on the penultimate syllable. The native vocabulary of the language does not tolerate final light syllables in non-function words. Consider the following examples of Spanish loans (the stress is appropriately marked both in the Spanish input and in the Huave output):

| Spanish | Huave | |
|---|---|---|
| kafé | kaféj | 'coffee' |
| potránka | potrán | 'filly' |
| kutʃíʎo | kotʃíl | 'knife' |
| garabáto | garabát | 'hook' |
| tixéras | tiʃér | 'scissors' |
| kardúmen | kardóm | 'flock' |
| ígado | ík | 'liver' |
| todabía | todabíj | 'still' |

(i)   Comment on the ways in which Huave preserves the Spanish stress input by accommodating it to the native constraints.

Apart from the constraints Max-IO and Dep-IO, the following constraints will be appropriate for your analysis:

MATCH<sub>STRESS</sub>:   Stress falls on the same vowel in the source word as in the loan word.

STRESS:   Cover term for constraints producing the Huave stress pattern.

FREE-V:   *V<sub>WORD</sub>] (No word-final open syllables.)

(ii)   Work out an appropriate constraint ranking.

(iii)   Demonstrate how your constraint ranking accounts for each of the forms listed above.

(Hint: in order to take into account all reasonable candidates you will need to postulate a further constraint not mentioned above.)

# EXERCISE 10:10   Faroese Stressed Vowels

The data below show that Faroese stressed vowels are lengthened in (a) but not in (b) (long vowels are represented by "ː", whereas long consonants are represented as geminates):

a.
| | |
|---|---|
| [víː] | 'as well' |
| [dúːn] | 'roaring noise' |
| [ʃíːp] | 'ship' |
| [éːta] | 'eat' |
| [lúːa] | 'to hang down' |
| [fléːa] | 'to roof with turf' |
| [múːnʊr] | 'difference' |
| [féːprɪ] | 'fever' (dat.) |
| [súːkrɪ] | 'sugar' (dat.) |
| [éːplɪ] | 'potato' |
| [véːtrɪ] | 'winter' (dat.) |
| [ʧéːtɪl] | 'kettle' (nom.) |
| [míːklɪr] | 'great' (masc. pl.) |

b.
| | |
|---|---|
| [négv] | 'much' |
| [ménn] | 'men' |
| [ʃíps] | 'ship's' |
| [lánd̥] | 'land' |
| [ég̊g̊] | 'egg' |
| [nɔtt] | 'night' |
| [fɔss] | 'waterfall' |
| [héndʊr] | 'hands' |
| [véstur] | 'west' |
| [gáffɪl] | 'fork' |
| [hʊ́ksa] | 'to think' |
| [ʧétlɪ] | 'kettle' (dat.) |
| [átli] | (a name) |

Work out the constraints which will account for the location of the stressed syllables and for the lengthening of the vowels. (Hint: you don't need to restrict yourself to the constraints reported on in the literature.)

# EXERCISE 10:11   **Sundanese Liquids**

Sundanese is an Austronesian language spoken in Western Java. In this language the form of the plural affix alternates between *-ar* and *-al*. This alternation is dependent on the occurrence of the liquids [l] and [r] in the root. In cases where neither liquid occurs in the root the affix surfaces as *-ar*, so it can reasonably be assumed that *-ar* is the underlying form of this affix.

a.   c-al-ombrek        'cold'              b.   ŋ-ar-ajlən        'jump'
     m-al-otret         'take a picture'         ŋ-ar-oplok        'flop down'
     b-al-ocor          'leaking'                g-ar-ətol         'diligent'
     s-al-iduru         'sit by a fire'          m-ar-ahal         'expensive'

From these data we can see that the feature [lateral] undergoes a form of dissimilation which can be attributed to the effects of the OCP. Using the constraints proposed below, work out the appropriate ranking to ensure that the correct candidate emerges as optimal.

OCP[lateral]
IDENT[lateral]
    (correspondent segments in the Input and Output have identical values
    for [lateral])
No-GAP
    (forbids the configuration *C   C   C)
                                      \   /
                                       F

## EXERCISE Double Reduplication in 10:12 Northern Lushootseed

The Puget Salish language Northern Lushootseed of British Columbia exhibits an interesting pattern of double reduplication, which we illustrate with the interaction of the diminutive and distributive morphemes with the stem in the following forms:

| | | | |
|---|---|---|---|
| a. | bədáʔ | 'child, offspring' | |
| b. | bí-badaʔ | 'small child' | DIMINUTIVE |
| c. | bəd-badáʔ | 'children' | DISTRIBUTIVE |
| d. | bí-bəd-badaʔ | 'dolls, litter (of animals)' | DIM-DIST |
| e. | bí-bi-badaʔ | 'young children' | DIST-DIM |

(i)   Work out how to get the form of the diminutive morpheme.

(ii)   Work out how to get the form of the distributive morpheme.

(iii)   How would you account for the two variants of the distributive morpheme?

In (f) and (g) below we add some competing candidates to those in (d) and (e) above:

f.   bí-bə-badaʔ
bíd-bə-badaʔ
bí-bəd-badaʔ
bíb-bəd-badaʔ

g.   bí-bid-badaʔ
bíd-bid-badaʔ
bíb-bi-badaʔ
bí-bi-badaʔ

(iv)   Determine the ranking for the following constraints and evaluate the candidates:

MAX-DIM:   Every element in the base has a correspondent in the diminutive reduplicant.

MAX-DIST:   Every element in the base has a correspondent in the distributive reduplicant.

OCP:   Adjacent identical elements are prohibited at the melodic level.

NOLINK:   No gemination. This constraint forbids the configuration X   X

$$\underset{F}{\bigvee}$$

NOCODA

(v)   Display your rankings in the form of a tableau.

# EXERCISE Klamath Distributive
# 10:13 Reduplication

In the examples of reduplication we have looked at so far, the form of the reduplicant morpheme is to a greater or lesser degree faithful to the form of the base, and the base is more or less faithful to the form of the input. Now consider the examples in (a) and (b) below. These are taken from the Oregon language Klamath, which provided the data for exercise 8:2 above.

a.  | *Input* | *Output* | |
|---|---|---|
| /DIST+mbodjˀ+dk/ | mbo-mpditk | 'wrinkled up' (dist.) |
| /DIST+smˀoqˀj+dk/ | smˀo-smqˀitk | 'having a mouthful' (dist.) |
| /DIST+pniw+abcˀ+a/ | pni-pnoːpcˀa | 'blow out' (dist.) |
| /DIST+poliː+kˀa/ | po-pliːkˀa | 'little policemen' (dist.) |

b.  | /DIST+dmesga/ | de-dməsga | 'seize' (dist.) |
|---|---|---|
| /DIST+sipc+a/ | si-səpca | 'put out a fire' (dist.) |
| /DIST+ɢatdkˀ+a/ | ɢa-ɢəttkˀa | 'are cold' (dist.) |
| /DIST+pikca+ʔaːkˀ/ | pi-pəkcaʔaːk | 'little pictures' (dist.) |

(i)   What is the reduplicant exhibiting faithfulness to?

(ii)  How does the correspondence model we have been assuming so far need to be extended?

# EXERCISE 10:14 Tagalog Infixation

In Tagalog, the main language of the Philippines, the position of the actor or trigger affix -*um*- is determined by the shape of the root to which it attaches. Thus, as we show in the small sample below, it may either occur as a prefix or as an infix:

| Root | Actor/trigger | |
|------|---------------|---|
| aral | um-aral | 'teach' |
| alis | um-alis | 'leave, go away' |
| uwi | um-uwi | 'go home' |
| sulat | s-um-ulat | 'write' |
| pasok | p-um-asok | 'enter' |
| ganda | g-um-anda | 'become beautiful' |
| gradwet | gr-um-adwet | 'graduate' |

(i)   What accounts for the position of the morpheme -*um*-?

(ii)  Which constraints can be called upon to account for the correct placement of -*um*-?

(iii) Show in the form of tableaux how the optimal candidate triumphs in each of the above forms.

# EXERCISE 10:15 Ulwa Infixation

In the Nicaraguan language Ulwa, the possessed form of a noun is formed by the affixation of a morpheme *ka*. This morpheme may behave either as a suffix or as an infix, as we can see from the data below:

| | Unsuffixed | Possessed | |
|---|------------|-----------|---|
| a. | ál | ál-ka | 'man' |
| | bás | bás-ka | 'hair' |
| | kíː | kíː-ka | 'stone' |
| | saná | saná-ka | 'deer' |
| | amák | amák-ka | 'bee' |
| | sapáː | sapáː-ka | 'forehead' |

b.   súːlu          súː-ka-lu        'dog'
     kúhbil         kúh-ka-bil       'knife'
     báskarna       bás-ka-karna     'comb'
     siwának        siwá-ka-nak      'root'
     anáːlaaka      anáː-ka-laaka    'chin'
     karásmak       karás-ka-mak     'knee'

Propose the alignment constraint(s) that will ensure the correct placement of the affix.

<hr>

## EXERCISE 10:16   Shona Height Harmony

The Central Bantu language Shona, spoken in Zimbabwe, exhibits the conflict between markedness and identity constraints. The language has a simple five-vowel system:

     i              u
        e        o
           a

The language exhibits height harmony affecting high and mid vowels, but in which the low vowel [a] does not participate. In (a) and (b) below we show the alternation between a high and a nonhigh vowel at work (-*a* is the "final vowel" morpheme all through):

a.   *Root+applicative suffix /Vr/*
     per-a          'end'            per-er-a         'end in'
     tʂet-a         'stick'          tʂet-er-a        'stick to'
     son-a          'sew'            son-er-a         'sew for'
     pon-a          'give birth'     pon-er-a         'give birth at'

b.   ip-a           'be evil'        ip-ir-a          'be evil for'
     ɓat-a          'hold'           ɓat-ir-a         'hold for'
     ʋaʋ-a          'itch'           ʋaʋ-ir-a         'itch at'
     ʂetuk-a        'jump'           ʂetuk-ir-a       'jump in'
     pofomadz-a     'blind'          pofomadz-ir-a    'blind for'

We know from the markedness statements that [+high] vowels are unmarked whereas [−high, −low] vowels are marked. Therefore we would expect the high variant in the suffix to triumph every time. Clearly some other constraint must intervene to ensure that from time to time the mid variant emerges. Show how the appropriate ranking of the following constraints will ensure that the correct candidate wins in *per-era, ip-ira, vav-ira, şetuk-ira* and *pofomadz-ira.*

> *MID
> > (No mid vowels)
>
> *HIGH
> > (No high vowels)
>
> IDENT[high]
> IDENTσ₁[high]
> > (Input–output identity for root initial syllable vowels for [high])
>
> IDENT[phar]
> > (Input–output identity for [pharyngeal] = [a])
>
> NOGAP
> > (forbids a configuration *V   V   V)
> > > F

# References

[1]     Ao, B. 1991: Kikongo Nasal Harmony and Context Sensitive Underspecification. *Linguistic Inquiry* 22, 193–97.

[2]     Aronoff, M. & Sridhar, S. 1988: Prefixation in Kannada. In M. Hammond & M. Noonan (eds), 1988: *Theoretical Morphology*. San Diego, CA: Academic Press, 179–91.

[3]     Beckman, J. 1996: Shona Height Harmony: Markedness and Positional Identity. In J. Beckman, L. Walsh Dickey & S. Urbanczyk (eds), *Papers in Optimality Theory*. University of Massachusetts Occasional Papers 18, UMass, Amherst: GLSA, 53–76.

[4]     Blevins, J. 1995: The Syllable in Phonological Theory. In J. Goldsmith (1995), 206–44.

[5]     Booij G. 1996: *The Phonology of Dutch*. Oxford: Clarendon Press.

[6]     Booij G. & Rubach, J. 1984: Morphological and Prosodic Domains. *Phonology Yearbook* 1, 1–24.

[7]     Borowsky, T. 1993: On the Word Level. In S. Hargus & E. Kaisse (1993), 199–234.

[8]     Brandão de Carvalho, J. 1997: Primitives et naturalité. *Langages* 125, 14–34.

[9]     Bravić, Z. 1988: Accent Systems in Croatian Dialects. In H. van der Hulst & N. Smith (eds), *Autosegmental Studies in Pitch Accent*. Dordrecht: Foris, 1–10.

[10]    Brown, G. 1972: *Phonological Rules and Dialect Variation: A Study of the Phonology of Lumasaaba*. Cambridge: Cambridge University Press.

[11]    Calabrese A. 1988: Towards a Theory of Phonological Alphabets. Ph.D., MIT.

[12]    Casali R. 1995: Labial Opacity and Roundness Harmony in Nawuri. *Natural Language and Linguistic Theory* 13, 649–63.

[13]    Chen, M. 1996: Tone Sandhi. MS, University of California, San Diego.

[14]    Cho, Y.-M. 1990: Syntax and Phrasing in Korean. In S. Inkelas & D. Zec (1990), 47–62.

[15]    Chung, S. 1983: Transderivational Relationships in Chamorro. *Language* 59, 35–65.

[16]    Clements, G. N. 1997: Berber Syllabification: Derivations or Constraints? In I. Roca (ed.), *Derivations and Constraints in Phonology*. Oxford: Clarendon Press, 289–330.

[17]    Clements, G. N. & Goldsmith, J. (eds) 1984: *Autosegmental Studies in Bantu Tone*. Dordrecht: Foris.

[18]    Clements, G. N. & Keyser, S. J. 1983: *CV Phonology*. Cambridge, MA: MIT Press.

[19]    Cole, J. & Kuo, F.-I. 1991: Phonological Enhancement in the Vowel Assimilation of Feʔ Feʔ Bamileke. *Chicago Linguistic Society* 27, 85–99.

[20]   Davidson L. & Noyer R. 1997: Loan Phonology in Huave. *West Coast Conference in Formal Linguistics* 15, 65–80.
[21]   Dell, F. 1985: *Les Règles et les Sons*. Paris: Hermann.
[22]   Dell, F. & Elmedlaoui, M. 1985: Syllabic Consonants and Syllabification in Imdlawn Tashlhiyt Berber. *Journal of African Language and Linguistics* 7, 105–30.
[23]   Dell, F. & Elmedlaoui, M. 1988: Syllabic Consonants in Berber: Some New Evidence. *Journal of African Language and Linguistics* 10, 1–17.
[24]   Durand, J. & Katamba, F. (eds) 1995: *Frontiers in Phonology*. London: Longman.
[25]   Gnanadesikan, A. 1995: Markedness and Faithfulness Constraints in Child Phonology. ROA-67.
[26]   Goldsmith, J. 1990: *Autosegmental and Metrical Phonology*. Oxford: Blackwell.
[27]   Goldsmith, J. (ed.) 1995: *The Handbook of Phonological Theory*. Oxford: Blackwell.
[28]   Hale, K. 1973: Deep and Surface Canonical Disparities in Relation to Analysis and Change: An Australian Example. In T. Sebeok (ed.), *Current Trends in Linguistics 9*. The Hague: Mouton, 401–58.
[29]   Hall, T. 1989: Lexical Phonology and the Distribution of German [ç] and [x]. *Phonology* 6, 1–18.
[30]   Halle, M. & Mohanan, K. P. 1985: Segmental Phonology of Modern English. *Linguistic Inquiry* 16, 57–116.
[31]   Halle, M. & Vergnaud, J.-R. 1981: Harmony Processes. In W. Klein & W. Levelt (eds), *Crossing the Boundaries in Linguistics*. Dordrecht: Reidel, 1–22.
[32]   Halle, M. & Vergnaud, J.-R. 1987: *An Essay on Stress*. Cambridge, MA: MIT Press.
[33]   Haraguchi, S. 1977: *The Tone Pattern of Japanese: An Autosegmental Theory of Tonology*. Tokyo: Kaitakusha.
[34]   Hargus, S. & Kaisse, E. (eds) 1993: *Studies in Lexical Phonology*. San Diego, CA: Academic Press.
[35]   Hashimoto, A. O. 1972: *Studies in Yue Dialects I: Phonology of Cantonese*. Cambridge: Cambridge University Press.
[36]   Hayes, B. 1980: *A Metrical Theory of Stress Rules*. Ph.D., MIT. New York: Garland, 1985.
[37]   Hayes, B. 1995: *Metrical Stress Theory: Principles and Case Studies*. Chicago: The University of Chicago Press.
[38]   Holton, D. 1996: Assimilation and Dissimilation of Sundanese Liquids. In J. Beckman, L. Walsh Dickey & S. Urbanczyk (eds), *Papers in Optimality Theory*. University of Massachusetts Occasional Papers 18, UMass, Amherst: GLSA, 167–80.
[39]   Hualde, J. 1991: *Basque Phonology*. London: Routledge.
[40]   Hulst, H. van der & Smith, N. 1982: Prosodic Domains and Opaque Segments in Autosegmental Phonology. In H. van der Hulst & N. Smith (eds), *The Structure of Phonological Representations*, vol. II. Dordrecht: Foris, 311–36.
[41]   Hume, E. 1990: Front Vowels, Palatal Consonants and the Rule of Umlaut in Korean. *North Eastern Linguistics Society* 20, 230–43.
[42]   Hyman, L. 1975: *Phonology Theory and Analysis*. New York: Holt, Rinehart and Winston.
[43]   Inkelas, S. & Zec, D. (eds) 1990: *The Phonology–Syntax Connection*. Chicago: The University of Chicago Press.
[44]   Itô, J. 1984: Melodic Dissimilation in Ainu. *Linguistic Inquiry* 15, 505–13.
[45]   Itô, J. 1986: Syllable Theory in Prosodic Phonology. Ph.D., University of Massachusetts at Amherst.
[46]   Jones, D. & Ward, D. 1969: *The Phonetics of Russian*. London: Cambridge University Press.

[47]  Kager, R. 1997: Generalised Alignment and Morphological Parsing. *Rivista di Linguistica* 9, 245–82. Also ROA-36.
[48]  Katada, F. 1990: On the Representation of Moras: Evidence from a Language Game. *Linguistic Inquiry* 21, 641–5.
[49]  Katamba, F. 1995: Skeleta and the Prosodic Circumscription of Morphological Domains. In J. Durand & F. Katamba (1995), 222–64.
[50]  Katz, D. 1987: *A Grammar of the Yiddish Language.* London: Duckworth.
[51]  Kenstowicz, M. 1994: *Phonology in Generative Grammar.* Oxford: Blackwell.
[52]  Kenstowicz, M. & Kisseberth, C. 1979: *Generative Phonology.* Orlando, FL: Academic Press.
[53]  Kiparsky, P. 1982: The Lexical Phonology of Vedic Sanskrit. MS, MIT.
[54]  Kisseberth, C. 1972: An Argument Against the Principle of Simultaneous Application of Phonological Rules. *Linguistic Inquiry* 3, 393–6.
[55]  Ladefoged, P. 1968: *A Phonetic Study of West African Languages.* Cambridge: Cambridge University Press.
[56]  Leben, W. 1984: Tone Alternations in Nzema. In M. Aronoff & R. Oehrle (eds), *Language Sound Structure.* Cambridge, MA: MIT Press, 137–44.
[57]  Lombardi, L. 1990: The Nonlinear Organisation of the Affricate. *Natural Language and Linguistic Theory* 8, 375–425.
[58]  McCarthy, J. & Prince, A. 1993: Generalised Alignment. *Yearbook in Morphology 1993.* Dordrecht: Kluwer, 79–153.
[59]  McCarthy, J. & Prince, A. 1995: Faithfulness and Reduplicative Identity. In J. Beckman, L. Walsh Dickey & S. Urbanczyk (eds), *Papers in Optimality Theory. University of Massachusetts Occasional Papers* 18, UMass, Amherst: GLSA, 249–384.
[60]  Méla, V. 1991: Le Verlan ou le Langage du Miroir. *Langages* 101, 73–94.
[61]  Mester, A. 1988: Dependent Tier Ordering and the OCP. In H. van der Hulst & N. Smith (eds), *Features, Segmental Structures & Harmony Processes,* Part II. Dordrecht: Foris, 127–44.
[62]  Mohanan, K. P. 1986: *The Theory of Lexical Phonology.* Dordrecht: Reidel.
[63]  Nespor, M. & Vogel, I. 1986: *Prosodic Phonology.* Dordrecht: Foris.
[64]  Odden, D. 1984: Stem Tone Assignment in Shona. In G. N. Clements & J. Goldsmith (1984), 255–80.
[65]  Odden, D. 1991: Vowel Geometry. *Phonology* 8, 261–89.
[66]  Padgett, J. 1994: Stricture and Nasal Place Assimilation. *Natural Language and Linguistic Theory* 12, 465–513.
[67]  Pike, K. 1948: *Tone Languages.* Ann Arbor: University of Michigan Press.
[68]  Poser, W. 1989: The Metrical Foot in Diyari. *Phonology* 6, 117–48.
[69]  Prince, A. 1983: Relating to the Grid. *Linguistic Inquiry* 14, 19–100.
[70]  Pulleyblank, D. 1986: *Tone in Lexical Phonology:* Dordrecht: Reidel.
[71]  Pulleyblank, D. 1995: Feature Geometry and Underspecification. In J. Durand & F. Katamba (1995), 3–33.
[72]  Rennison, J. 1986: On Tridirectional Feature Systems for Vowels. In J. Durand (ed.), *Dependency and Non-Linear Phonology.* London: Croom Helm, 281–304.
[73]  Rice, K. 1990: Predicting Rule Domains in the Phrasal Phonology. In S. Inkelas & D. Zec (1990), 289–312.
[74]  Roca, I. 1994: *Generative Phonology.* London: Routledge.
[75]  Rubach, J. 1984: *Cyclic and Lexical Phonology: The Structure of Polish.* Dordrecht: Foris.
[76]  Rubach, J. 1993: *The Lexical Phonology of Slovak.* Oxford: Clarendon Press.
[77]  Rubach, J. 1995: Representations and Rules in Slavic Phonology. In J. Goldsmith (1995), 848–66.

[78]  Rubach, J. & Booij, G. 1990: Syllable Structure Assignment in Polish. *Phonology* 7, 121–58.

[79]  Sagey, E. 1986: The Representation of Features and Relations in Non-Linear Phonology. Ph.D., MIT. New York: Garland, 1991.

[80]  Schachter, P. & Otanes, F. T. 1972: *Tagalog Reference Grammar*. Berkeley, CA: University of California Press.

[81]  Schachter, P. & Fromkin, V. 1968: *A Phonology of Akan: Akuapem, Asante & Fante*. *Working Papers in Phonetics* 9, University of California, Los Angeles.

[82]  Selkirk, E. 1972: The Phrase Phonology of English and French. Ph.D., University of Massachusetts at Amherst. Distributed by the Indiana University Linguistics Club. New York: Garland, 1980.

[83]  Shaw, P. 1991: Consonant Harmony Systems. In C. Paradis & J.-F. Prunet (eds), *The Special Status of Coronals: Internal and External Evidence*. San Diego, CA: Academic Press, 125–57.

[84]  Smith, N. 1973: *The Acquisition of Phonology*. Cambridge: Cambridge University Press.

[85]  Steriade, D. 1987: Redundant Values. In A. Bosch et al. (eds), *Parasession of Autosegmental and Metrical Phonology*, Chicago Linguistic Society, 339–62.

[86]  Tsujimura, N. 1996: *An Introduction to Japanese Linguistics*. Oxford: Blackwell.

[87]  *Twi Basic Course*. Washington, DC: Foreign Service Institute.

[88]  Urbanczyk, S. 1995: Double Reduplication in Parallel. In J. Beckman, L. Walsh Dickey & S. Urbanczyk (eds), *Papers in Optimality Theory*. University of Massachusetts Occasional Papers 18, UMass, Amherst: GLSA, 499–532.

[89]  Vennemann, T. 1978: Universal Syllable Phonology. *Theoretical Linguistics* 5, 175–214.

[90]  Yip, M. 1994: Isolated Uses of Prosodic Categories. In J. Cole & C. Kisseberth (eds), *Perspectives in Phonology*. Stanford, CA: CLSI Publications, 293–308.

[91]  Zaharani-Ahmad 1998: Phonology and Morphology Interface in Malay: An Optimality-Theoretic Account. Ph.D., University of Essex.

[92]  Zec, D. 1995: The Role of Moraic Structure on the Distribution of Segments within Syllables. In J. Durand & F. Katamba (1995), 149–79.

# Language Details

[NB: Information about the death of a language is not always readily available.]

| Name | Family | Area where spoken | Exercise no. |
|---|---|---|---|
| Ainu | isolate | [near extinct] Hokkaido (Japan); Sakhalin & Kurile Islands (Russia) | 8:5 |
| Akan | Kwa (Niger-Congo) | Ghana; Ivory Coast | 2:7 |
| Anxiang | Sinic (Sino-Tibetan) | Hunan (PR China) | 3:7 |
| Bahasa Melayu/ Indonesian | W Malayo-Polynesian (Austronesian) | Malaysia; Indonesia; Brunei; Singapore | 10:3 |
| Bamileke see Feʔ Feʔ Bamileke | | | |
| Basque | isolate | Basque Country & N Navarre (N Spain); adjacent territories in France | 5:6 |
| Berber | Afro-Asiatic | Morocco; Algeria; other territories in Northern Africa | 3:10 |
| Cantonese | Sinic (Sino-Tibetan) | Guangdong & Hong Kong (PR China) | 5:10 |
| Capanhua | Panoan | W South America | 8:8 |
| Chamorro | (Austronesian) | W Malayo-Polynesian Guam (USA) & other Mariana Is. | 6:5, 6:6 |
| Cheremis see Eastern Cheremis | | | |
| Creek | Muskogean | Oklahoma & Florida (USA) | 4:6 |
| Diola Fogny | Niger-Congo | Guinea-Bissau; Gambia | 3:8 |
| Diyari | Karnic (Australian) | S Australia | 7:7, 10:8 |
| Dutch | W Germanic (Indo-European) | Netherlands; Flanders (Belgium); Surinam | 2:3 |
| Eastern Cheremis | Finno-Volgaic (Uralic) | E Volga region (Russia) | 2:10 |
| English | W Germanic (Indo-European) | UK; USA; Canada; Australia; New Zealand; South Africa; former colonies | 2:11, 3:5, 4:1, 4:5, 7:4, 7:8, 10:1 |
| Faroese | N Germanic (Indo-European) | Faroe Islands (Denmark) | 10:10 |
| Feʔ Feʔ Bamileke | Bantu (Niger-Congo) | Cameroon | 8:10 |

| Name | Family | Area where spoken | Exercise no. |
|---|---|---|---|
| French | Romance (Indo-European) | France; Wallonia (Belgium); W Switzerland; Quebec (Canada); former colonies | 3:1 |
| German | W Germanic (Indo-European) | Germany; Austria; Switzerland; Luxemburg | 2:2, 3:3, 6:1 |
| Hindi | Indo-Aryan (Indo-European) | N & Central India | 4:7 |
| Huave | Penutian (North American) | Mexico | 10:9 |
| Hungarian | Finno-Ugric (Uralian) | Hungary; some adjacent territories | 7:6 |
| Icelandic | N Germanic (Indo-European) | Iceland | 3:6 |
| Italian | Romance (Indo-European) | Italy | 7:3, 7:5 |
| Japanese | isolate | Japan | 2:1, 2:9, 4:8, 5:5 |
| Kannada | S Dravidian | Mysore (India) | 2:6 |
| Kikongo | Bantu (Niger-Congo) | Democratic Republic of Congo | 8:9 |
| Klamath | Penutian (North American) | Oregon (USA) | 8:2, 10:13 |
| Korean | Altaic | N & S Korea | 7:2, 9:4 |
| Koromfe | Niger-Congo | Burkina Faso | 8:3 |
| Kutep | Niger-Congo | W Africa | 2:13 |
| Lenakel | Austronesian | Tanna Is. (Vanuatu) | 3:2, 4:4, 10:4 |
| Lumasaaba | Bantu (Niger-Congo) | Uganda | 8:1, 9:5 |
| Lushootseed | Puget-Salish | British Columbia (Canada) | 10:12 |
| Malay see Bahasa Melayu/Indonesian | | | |
| Malayalam | S Dravidian | Kerala & Laccadive Is. (India) | 4:9 |
| Mixtecan | Oto-Manguean | Oaxaca (Mexico) | 5:2 |
| Nawuri | Kwa (Niger-Congo) | Ghana | 8:4 |
| Ngbaka | Ubangi (Niger-Congo) | Democratic Republic of Congo | 8:6 |
| Nzema | Volta-Comoe | Ghana; Ivory Coast | 5:8 |
| Pali | Indo-Aryan (Indo-European) | [extinct] language of the Theravādin Buddhist canon | 3:4, 10:2 |
| Pintupi | Pama-Nyungan | Australia | 4:3, 10:6 |
| Polish | W Slavic (Indo-European) | Poland | 6:3, 8:7, 10:5 |
| Ponapean | E Malayo-Polynesian (Austronesian) | Ponape Is. | 6:2 |
| Russian | E Slavic (Indo-European) | Russia and outposts | 4:2 |
| Sanskrit | Indo-Aryan (Indo-European) | [evolved] India | 6:4 |
| Sea Dayak | W Malayo-Polynesian (Austronesian) | E Borneo (Sarawak, Malaysia) | 9:1 |

| Name | Family | Area where spoken | Exercise no. |
|---|---|---|---|
| Serbo-Croatian | S Slavic (Indo-European) | Serbia; Croatia; Bosnia-Herzegovenia; Montenegro | 5:4 |
| Shona | Bantu (Niger-Congo) | Zimbabwe | 5:9, 10:16 |
| Slave | Athapaskan | Canada | 7:1 |
| Slovak | W Slavic (Indo-European) | Slovakia | 2:14 |
| Spanish | Romance (Indo-European) | Spain; former colonies (particularly in the Americas) | 2:5 |
| Sundanese | W Malayo-Polynesian (Austronesian) | W Java (Indonesia) | 10:11 |
| Tahltan | Athapaskan | British Columbia (Canada) | 2:8 |
| Tübatulabal | Uto-Aztecan | [near extinct] S California (USA) | 4:10 |
| Tunica | Penutian (North American) | [extinct] Gulf of Mexico (USA) | 9:2 |
| Turkish | Turkic (Altaic) | Turkey; N Cyprus | 3:9 |
| Ulwa | Sumu (Macro-Chibchan) | Nicaragua | 10:15 |
| Venda | Bantu (Niger-Congo) | South Africa | 5:3 |
| Yala Ikom | Kwa (Niger-Congo) | Nigeria | 5:1 |
| Yawelmani | Penutian (North American) | [extinct] Central Valley of California (USA) | 9:6 |
| Yiddish | W Germanic (Indo-European) | Central and Eastern Europe; USA; Israel | 2:4 |
| Yoruba | Defoid (Niger-Congo) | SW Nigeria; Benin; Togo | 5:7 |
| Zoque | Mixe-Zoquean | S Mexico | 2:12 |

# Exercise Cross-Reference Table

**Key:**
D    = Data (source of the data in the exercise)
A    = Analysis (the paper contains an analysis of the data)
C    = Comment (the data are commented on and discussed in the paper)
[00] = Number associated with the work in the list of references
[A]  = Data provided by the authors

| Exercise number | Relevant chapter (section) in *A Course in Phonology* | D | A | C | Exercise title |
|---|---|---|---|---|---|
| 1:1 | 1 | | | | Articulation and Phonetic Symbols |
| 1:2 | 1 | | | | Ghoti Words |
| 1:3 | 1 | | | | Incomplete Diagrams |
| 1:4 | 3 | | | | Place and Manner of Articulation |
| 1:5 | 3 | | | | Glottal Stops and Flaps |
| 1:6 | 5,7 | | | | Cardinal Vowels |
| 1:7 | 7 | | | | English Vowels |
| 1:8 | 7 | | | | Vowels |
| 1:9 | 7 | | | | RP Phonetic Transcription |
| 1:10 | 7 | | | | GA Phonetic Transcription |

| Exercise number | Relevant chapter (section) in *A Course in Phonology* | D | A | C | Exercise title |
|---|---|---|---|---|---|
| 1:11 | 7 | | | | Transcription from Orthography to Phonetics |
| 1:12 | 5 | | | | Nonsense Words |
| 1:13 | 7 | | | | GA Phonetic Transcription |
| 1:14 | 7 | | | | RP Phonetic Transcription |
| 1:15 | 7 | | | | Faulty Transcription |
| | | | | | |
| 2:1 | 2(5) | [86] | | [86] | Japanese |
| 2:2 | 2(5) | [A] | | | German Obstruents |
| 2:3 | 2(3,6) | [5] | | [5] | Dutch Past Tense Suffix |
| 2:4 | 2(3,6) | [50] | | | Yiddish |
| 2:5 | 4 | [A] | | | Spanish |
| 2:6 | 4(7,8) | [2] | [2] | | Kannada Prefixation |
| 2:7 | 6(3,4) | [11] [31] [81] [87] | [31] | [11] | Akan Vowel Harmony |
| 2:8 | 6 | [71] [83] | [71] [83] | | Tahltan Coronals |
| 2:9 | 6(1,2) | [86] | | [86] | Japanese Again |
| 2:10 | 6(3,4) | [65] | [65] | | Eastern Cheremis |
| 2:11 | 6 | [84] | | | A Child's Language |
| 2:12 | 8(1,9) | [21] [57] [79] [85] | [79] [85] | [21] [57] | Zoque |
| 2:13 | 8(1,9) | [55] [79] | [79] | | Kutep |
| 2:14 | 8(4) | [76] [77] | [76] | | Slovak Vowel Length |
| | | | | | |

| Exercise number | Relevant chapter (section) in *A Course in Phonology* | D | A | C | Exercise title |
|---|---|---|---|---|---|
| 3:1 | 9(4) | [60] | | | A French Language Game |
| 3:2 | 9 | [4] | [4] | | Lenakel Epenthesis |
| 3:3 | 9 | [A] | | | German Again |
| 3:4 | 9 | [92] | [92] | | Pali |
| 3:5 | 9,10 | [A] | | | English Vowel Deletion |
| 3:6 | 10(1) | [45] [51] | [45] | | Icelandic |
| 3:7 | 10 | [90] | [90] | | Anxiang Suffixation |
| 3:8 | 10(9) | [45] | [45] | | Diola Fogny |
| 3:9 | 10 | [18] | [18] | | Turkish |
| 3:10 | 10 | [16] [22] [23] | [22] [23] | | Berber Syllabification |
| | | | | | |
| 4:1 | 11(9) | [A] | | | English Rhythm |
| 4:2 | 11(10) | [46] | | | Russian Vowel Distribution |
| 4:3 | 12(10) | [37] | [37] | | Pintupi |
| 4:4 | 12(10) | [40] [37] | [37] | | Lenakel Stress |
| 4:5 | 13(2) | [A] | | | The English Stress Algorithm |
| 4:6 | 13 | [26] [37] [69] | [26] [37] [69] | | Creek |
| 4:7 | 13 | [36] [37] | [36] [37] | | Hindi |
| 4:8 | 13(5) | [48] | [48] | | A Japanese Language Game |
| 4:9 | 13(8) | [37] [62] | [37] | [62] | Stress in Malayalam |
| 4:10 | 13(9) | [37] [69] | [37] [69] | | Tübatulabal |
| | | | | | |

| Exercise number | Relevant chapter (section) in *A Course in Phonology* | D | A | C | Exercise title |
|---|---|---|---|---|---|
| 5:1 | 14(11) | [70] | [70] | | Yala Ikom Reduplication |
| 5:2 | 14(12) | [26] [67] | | [26] | Mixtecan |
| 5:3 | 14(11) | [51] | [51] | | Venda Tones |
| 5:4 | 14(10) | [9] | [9] | | Croatian Dialects |
| 5:5 | 14(10) | [33] | [33] | | Osaka Japanese |
| 5:6 | 14(10) | [39] | [39] | | Gernika Basque Pitch Accent |
| 5:7 | 14(11) | [70] | [70] | | Yoruba |
| 5:8 | 14(12) | [56] | [56] | | Nzema |
| 5:9 | 14(11) | [64] | [64] | | Karanga Shona |
| 5:10 | 14(9) | [13] [35] | [13] | | Cantonese |
| | | | | | |
| 6:1 | 16 | [29] | [29] | [7] | German |
| 6:2 | 15(5) | [45] | | [45] | Ponapean |
| 6:3 | 15 | [6] [75] | [6] [75] | | Polish |
| 6:4 | 16 | [30] [53] | [30] [53] | [32] [74] | Vedic Sanskrit |
| 6:5 | 15,16 | [15] | [15] [32] | | Chamorro Stress Assignment |
| 6:6 | 15,16 | [15] | [15] [32] | | Chamorro Secondary Stress |
| | | | | | |
| 7:1 | 16 | [73] | [73] | | Slave |
| 7:2 | 16 | [14] | [14] | | Korean Obstruent Voicing |
| 7:3 | 16(10) | [63] | [63] | | Italian Stress Retraction |
| 7:4 | 16 | [63] [74] [82] | [63] | [74] | English Sandhi |

| Exercise number | Relevant chapter (section) in *A Course in Phonology* | D | A | C | Exercise title |
|---|---|---|---|---|---|
| 7:5 | 16(11) | [63] | [63] | | Tuscan Italian |
| 7:6 | 16 | [63] | [63] | | The Phonological Word in Hungarian |
| 7:7 | 16 | [32] [68] | [32] [68] | | Diyari Stress |
| 7:8 | 16 | [A] | | | English |
| | | | | | |
| 8:1 | 17 | [10] | | | Lumasaaba |
| 8:2 | 17 | [54] | | | Klamath Glottalized Consonants |
| 8:3 | 17 | [72] | | [72] | Koromfe |
| 8:4 | 17 | [12] | [12] | | Vowel Harmony in Nawuri |
| 8:5 | 17 | [8] [44] [61] | [44] [61] | [8] | Ainu |
| 8:6 | 17 | [8] [44] [61] | [61] | [8] [44] | Ngbaka |
| 8:7 | 17 | [66] | [66] | | Polish Nasal Vowels |
| 8:8 | 17 | [31] [40] | [31] [40] | | Capanhua |
| 8:9 | 17 | [1] | [1] | | Kikongo Nasal Harmony |
| 8:10 | 17(11) | [19] | [19] | | Reduplication in Feʔ Feʔ Bamileke |
| | | | | | |
| 9:1 | 18(1,2) | [42] [52] | | [42] [52] | Sea Dayak |
| 9:2 | 18(1,2) | [52] | | [52] | Tunica |
| 9:3 | 18(1,2) | [52] | | [52] | Shona |
| 9:4 | 18 | [41] | [41] | | Rule Interaction in Korean |

| Exercise number | Relevant chapter (section) in *A Course in Phonology* | D | A | C | Exercise title |
|---|---|---|---|---|---|
| 9:5 | 18 | [10] | | | Lumasaaba |
| 9:6 | 18 | [21] [51] | [51] | | Yawelmani Vowel System |
| | | | | | |
| 10:1 | 19 | [25] | [25] | | A Child's Language |
| 10:2 | 19(5) | [92] | | | Pali Syllables |
| 10:3 | 19(6) | [91] | [91] | | Malay Syllable Structure |
| 10:4 | 19(5) | [4] | | | Lenakel Syllabification |
| 10:5 | 19(6) | [78] | | | Polish Onsets |
| 10:6 | 19(8) | [37] | | | Pintupi Stress |
| 10:7 | 19(8) | [58] | [58] | | Garawa Stress |
| 10:8 | 19 | [47] [69] | [47] | | Diyari Stress Again |
| 10:9 | 19(9) | [20] | [20] | | Syllable Weight and Syllable Count in Huave Loanwords |
| 10:10 | 19(9) | [89] | | | Faroese Stressed Vowels |
| 10:11 | 19 | [38] | [38] | | Sundanese Liquids |
| 10:12 | 19 | [88] | [88] | | Double Reduplication in Northern Lushootseed |
| 10:13 | 19 | [59] | [59] | | Klamath Distributive Reduplication |
| 10:14 | 19 | [58] [80] | [58] | | Tagalog Infixation |
| 10:15 | 19 | [49] [58] | [58] | | Ulwa Infixation |
| 10:16 | 19 | [3] | [3] | | Shona Height Harmony |

# Correspondences with
# *A Course in Phonology*

# Index